ENVIRONMENTAL ASSESSMENT - June 15, 2001

U.S. FISH AND WILDLIFE SERVICE, DEPARTMENT OF THE INTERIOR

ENVIRONMENTAL ASSESSMENT

PROPOSAL TO ESTABLISH OPERATIONAL/EXPERIMENTAL GENERAL SWAN HUNTING SEASONS IN THE PACIFIC FLYWAY

I.   PURPOSE AND NEED FOR ACTION

A.   BACKGROUND

Flyway Management Approach

In developing management actions for migratory game birds, the U.S. Fish and Wildlife Service (Service) has publicly supported the goals, objectives, and management strategies identified in the various Flyway management plans for both Tundra (*C. columbianus*) and Trumpeter (*C. buccinator*) swans (Hartwig 1989, Gritman 1991, Schmidt 2000). It has encouraged cooperative, multi-State-sponsored, Flyway Council-endorsed projects for restoring <u>migratory</u> flocks of Trumpeter swans within their historic range and has supported Flyway Council-endorsed hunting seasons on Tundra swans within prescribed guidelines that meet overall objectives for all swan populations.

The Service has previously recognized that there would be unauthorized killing of Trumpeter swans and others would be killed by hunters accidentally and incidental to regulated hunting seasons. Such accidental hunting losses are likely to remain proportional to size and distribution of Trumpeter swan populations. The Service believes that ongoing or new hunting programs, whether for Tundra swans or other waterfowl, should be neither curtailed nor prohibited because of the chance-killing of a Trumpeter swan when such taking has negligible impacts on achieving management objectives. Conversely, Tundra swan hunting should be restricted or not permitted at times of the season or in places where it would irreparably affect the status of a particular population of Trumpeter swans.

As policy (Hartwig 1989, Schmidt 2000), the Service supports the concept of Flyway management of waterfowl and gives strong consideration for Flyway Council-endorsed programs and recommendations. Therefore, the Flyway Councils have been urged to carefully examine impacts of waterfowl hunting programs on Trumpeter swan restoration efforts and vice versa and resolve conflicts early-on before making recommendations to the Service. Also, the Service will and must give consideration to the broad interests of all of the public in management of its migratory bird resources. When there are irreconcilable differences among States, Flyway Councils, and the public regarding appropriate management for Trumpeter and Tundra swans, the Service policy will be to deal with such issues on a case by case basis, investigate the biological implications and document the results of those investigations.

B.   NEED FOR THE PROPOSED ACTION

A legal season that also permitted the take of a limited number of Trumpeter swans in the Pacific Flyway was instituted in 1995.   Prior to that time and beginning in 1962 a Tundra swan season had been in effect. During the Tundra swan seasons it was known that some number of Trumpeter swans were taken by swan hunters who mistook them for Tundra swans. This limited take was authorized in an attempt to reconcile potentially conflicting strategies for managing two swan species in the Pacific Flyway. The potentially conflicting strategies are: (1) to enhance the winter range distribution of the less abundant Rocky Mountain Population (RMP) of Trumpeter swans by severely restricting or eliminating swan hunting in portions of the Pacific Flyway currently open to hunting these species, and (2) to continue to provide harvest opportunities of the more numerous and widely distributed Western Population (WP) of Tundra swans in the Pacific Flyway.

The Service issued a finding of no significant impact in August of 1995 and again in July of 2000 after assessing impacts in two previous Environmental Assessments on this issue (Bartonek et al. 1995, Trost et al. 2000). The proposed actions in these Environmental Assessments represented a balance between the two competing management strategies by establishing a general swan season in portions of Montana, Utah, and Nevada that allowed the taking of any species of swan (*Cygnus* sp.) subject to certain conditions:

(1)   a limited quota on the take of Trumpeter swans, which, upon being reached would trigger the cessation of all swan hunting in the designated area,

(2)   modification of the already limited take and restricted seasons on Tundra swans to enhance the likelihood that Trumpeter swans would be successful in expanding their winter range, and,

(3)   the development and implementation of a program to monitor the effectiveness of this action.

A review of the biological information from the five-year experimental period was recently completed and is included in the 2000 Supplemental Environmental Assessment (Trost et al. 2000). That review and subsequent Supplemental Environmental Assessment provided a summary of population, harvest and management activities derived from the experimental period available at that time. This review and assessment was relative to the original Environmental Assessment: Proposal to establish general swan hunting seasons in parts of the Pacific Flyway for the 1995-99 seasons (Bartonek et al. 1995). Since completion of the 2000 Supplemental Environmental Assessment, additional information regarding the population status of Trumpeter swans has become available. The Service believes this information is significant in assessing current management with regard to this issue and thus has chosen to develop this new Environmental Assessment to incorporate information gained during the most recent hunting season as well as the recent survey results from the periodic Continental Trumpeter swan survey and other sources.

This Environmental Assessment addresses public comments and concerns, including new and supplemental information gathered by the Service and cooperators during the past hunting season and during breeding and wintering surveys.   There is now a need to assess this new information and make a determination regarding the 2001-2002 and 2002-2003 swan hunting season in the Pacific Flyway.

C.   PURPOSE OF THE PROPOSED ACTION

The purpose of this proposed action is to establish regulatory options and management direction for Trumpeter and Tundra swans based on past experience with the authorization of a limited take of Trumpeter swans in the Pacific Flyway.

In addition, new information gathered over the past year will be used to reassess Trumpeter swan population status and the potential impact of a limited take of Trumpeter swans in the Pacific Flyway.

D.   SCOPE OF THE ENVIRONMENTAL ASSESSMENT

The geographic scope of the swan resource affected by this proposed action includes RMP Trumpeter swans, WP Tundra swans, and potentially feral mute swans (*C. olor*) should they occur in a hunt area. The geographic scope is restricted to portions of the States of Montana (only the Pacific Flyway portion), Utah, and Nevada where swans would be hunted. All States of the Pacific Flyway within the potential range of RMP Trumpeter swans (Fig. 1) would be included in potential management actions designed to enhance the status and distribution of this species.

The Service views the RMP of Trumpeter swans as a single management entity. However, due to concerns raised by the public, potential impacts on smaller groups of Trumpeter swans associated with specific areas, such as Yellowstone National Park and/or the Tristate Area (as defined below), will be discussed in this Environmental Assessment.

On August 22, 2000, the Service was petitioned to list a portion of the RMP of Trumpeter swans. The petitioners requested that the Service consider emergency listing of the Tristate flock. The Service acknowledged receipt of the petition and informed the petitioners that listing funds are not currently available for processing of administrative petition findings. Additionally, the Service stated that the population trend data for the RMP of Trumpeter swans indicated that there was no compelling evidence to indicate that emergency listing was appropriate.

The temporal scope of this proposed action is the 2001-2002 and 2002-2003 hunting seasons. The Service plans to review results with respect to both Tundra swan and Trumpeter swan harvests annually and proposed changes would be considered as a normal part of the annual hunting regulations process. The Service views the seasons in Montana and Nevada as operational seasons that are subject to the normal annual review of status and harvest of the affected populations. Adjustments to these seasons will be made, if needed, as part of the normal annual regulatory process for hunting migratory birds. As proposed here the season in Utah is experimental and will thus be fully reviewed at the conclusion of the 2002-2003 hunting season when a determination as to the acceptability of continuing the hunt will be made. At the conclusion of the experimental period, an assessment report will be prepared and the Service will determine the appropriate course of action for either continuation or suspension of this experimental season.   Procedures for issuance of annual regulations are found in SEIS

88, Final Supplemental Environmental Impact Statement: Issuance of annual regulations permitting the sport hunting of migratory birds (USDI 1988).

E. AUTHORITY AND RESPONSIBILITY

In the United States the preeminent authority and responsibility for migratory game birds lies with the Secretary of the Interior and is derived from international treaties to which the Constitution specifies that only the Federal Government can be signatory. The key instrument defining Federal authority is the Migratory Bird Treaty Act of 1918 (as amended). Among those species designated as "migratory game birds" for which there is Federal management authority is the taxonomic family *Anatidae*, which includes ducks, geese, brant, and swans. Authority for establishing hunting seasons for both Tundra and Trumpeter swans is provided in the Migratory Bird Treaty Act and appropriate Federal regulations (50 CFR). Regulations governing the establishment of annual regulations for the hunting of migratory birds are specified in *Title 50 Code of Federal Regulations, Part 20, Subpart K*. Any authorization of hunting or taking of swans or other migratory birds will be done in compliance with the Migratory Bird Treaty Act and associated regulations.

II. PROPOSED ACTION AND ALTERNATIVES

Actions Common to All Alternatives

Although not directly related to the issue of hunting seasons, the Service will continue to provide a leadership role in attempting to enhance Trumpeter swan status and breeding distribution within the Pacific Flyway through increased efforts directed at reestablishment of breeding Trumpeter swans in suitable habitats throughout the Pacific Flyway. The Service is currently funding the propagation of about 40 cygnets for future release into suitable habitat in the Tristate area.
The Service would also continue to support cooperative efforts to address the winter distribution issues by working with State, Non-governmental organizations (NGO) and individual partners. The Service would support limited winter capture and translocation on a case by case basis when circumstances developed that warrant such activity. The Service does not plan to employ winter translocations as the primary method to address the winter distribution problem of RMP Trumpeter swans. Rather translocation will be employed as a method to limit risk to swans from direct over-winter mortality, on an as needed basis.

Continued progress toward development and implementation of the requested implementation plan (Trost et al. 2000, FR Vol. 65, No. 188, pg 58517) has occurred. The Service has completed it's portion of this plan (Appendix A) and believes the actions outlined in this plan can help address concerns regarding the number of swans nesting in the Tristate area and help establish new winter distribution patterns. Evidence suggests current and past management activities have made progress toward improving the winter distribution situation (Bouffard 2000). We expect that further actions will continue to improve the status and distribution of RMP Trumpeter swans. Implementation efforts will be continued by the Service under each of the alternatives to the greatest extent possible.

A. ALTERNATIVE 1 (PREFERRED ALTERNATIVE) - ALLOW A LIMITED TAKE OF TRUMPETER SWANS DURING RESTRUCTURED SWAN HUNTING SEASONS:

The Service would continue to establish a hunting season for tundra swans with an authorization of a small take of trumpeter swans in designated portions of Montana, Utah and Nevada, within the Pacific Flyway. Constraints imposed upon swan hunting seasons described in the Supplemental Environmental Assessment on this issue (Trost et al. 2000) would be continued. Specific areas open to swan hunting in Montana, Utah and Nevada would remain as defined under the preferred alternative in the Supplemental Environmental Assessment on this issue (Trost et al. 2000). In general, the proposed action reduces and/or alters the areas open to swan hunting from the area that existed prior to the 1995 Environmental Assessment in Montana, Utah and Nevada as follows:

Montana: Beginning in 1995, those portions of Teton and Pondera Counties lying west of US Highway 287 from Augusta to Chouteau and west of US Highway 89 to the Blackfoot Indian Reservation were closed to all swan hunting. Chouteau County was added to the swan hunt area of the Pacific Flyway portion of Montana at this time. This area is proposed for continuation as the area open to swan hunting in Montana under this alternative.

Utah: Beginning in 1995, the swan hunt area in Utah was reduced from Statewide to a portion of the Great Salt Lake Basin and further reduced for the 2000-2001 hunting season. The area proposed for swan hunting is: Those portions of Box Elder, Weber, Davis, Salt Lake, and Toole Counties lying west of I-15, north of I-80, and south of a line beginning from the Forest Street exit to the Bear River Migratory Bird Refuge (BRMBR) boundary, then north and west along the BRMBR boundary to the farthest west boundary of the Refuge, then west along a line to Promontory Road, then north on Promontory Road to the intersection of SR-83, then north on SR-83 to I-84, then north and west on I-84 to State Hwy 30, then west on State Hwy 30 to the Nevada-Utah state line, then south on the Nevada-Utah state line to I-80.

Nevada: The area open to swan hunting in Nevada is Churchill, Pershing and Lyon Counties. This area was not altered in either of the preceding Environmental Assessments and is the area proposed for continuation of swan hunting under this alternative.

In addition to alterations in the areas open to swan hunting, changes in the number of Tundra swan permits and season closing dates were described in the previous Environmental Assessments (Bartonek et al.1995, Trost et al. 2000) and the Service proposes their continuation under this alternative as follows:

Montana: Season dates adjusted from the first Saturday in October to the Sunday closest to January 20 to the first Saturday in October to 1 December. Total swan permits to be issued remain unchanged at 500.

Utah: Season dates were adjusted from the first Saturday in October to the Sunday closest to January 20 to the first Saturday in October to the second Sunday in December. Permits were reduced from

2,500 to 2,000. [Note: the 1995 Environmental Assessment actually increased the permit number to 2,750, but mandated the season closure as the first Sunday in December, these provisions were modified in the 2000 Supplemental Environmental Assessment along with the additional area restrictions and the reduction in quota].

Nevada: Season dates were adjusted from the first Saturday in October to the Sunday closest to January 20 to the first Saturday in October to the Sunday following January 1. Permit numbers remained at 650. This alternative proposes to maintain these regulations.

Additionally, the Service would continue to require the monitoring of swan harvests, by mail in Montana, and by examination in Nevada and Utah, with appropriate provisions for season closure to be implemented by States should take of Trumpeters reach the assigned quotas. Quotas would be 10 in Utah and 5 in Nevada. The quota in Utah was reduced in the 2000 EA (from 15 to 10) in recognition of the fact that a total accounting of all dead Trumpeter swans could not be achieved and that based on reasonable estimates of reporting rates and losses to wounding, this reduction insured that these factors were taken into account in determining at what point to close the season to ensure protection of RMP Trumpeter swans. The number of swan hunting permits would not be altered from numbers issued in the 2000-2001 hunting season. Swan hunters will be required to have all harvested swans physically examined in Utah and Nevada within 72 hours of harvest. In Montana, hunters must submit required harvest information within seventy-two hours of harvesting a swan. The seventy-two hour time period is to allow for a reasonable time period for hunters to contact the necessary State or Federal staff to have a harvested swan examined. The Service will require Utah to enter into a Memorandum of Understanding (MOU) with the Service that agrees with the following further stipulations with regard to swan harvest monitoring in Utah: (1) Swans must be physically checked within seventy-two hours of harvest, (2) A commitment to enforce this regulation must be made by the State of Utah, (3) Utah hunters must hunt with their permit in their possession, and said permit must be validated with time and place a swan is killed prior to removing the swan from the field, (4) Adequate State provisions must be in place to effect a prompt season closure should the quota be reached, and (5) at a minimum, a weekly summary of swan harvests will be made to the Service and the Service will be immediately notified should the harvest quota be reached. The Service will not authorize a swan hunting season in Utah without such an MOU.

B.   ALTERNATIVE 2 - NO ACTION:

Under the No Action Alternative, the management scenario used prior to 1994 would be re-instituted. The Service would continue to establish open seasons on Tundra swans in all of Utah and parts of Montana and Nevada, while not allowing take of Trumpeter swans. There would be no closure of areas where Tundra and Trumpeter swans overlap in their fall/winter distribution.

Permits issued for take of Tundra swans would be set at 2,500 for Utah, 500 for Nevada and 650 for Montana. Season open and close dates would revert to those in place prior to the 1995 Environmental Assessment (Bartonek et al. 1995). These would be an opening framework date of the Saturday nearest October 1 and a closing date of the Sunday nearest January 20.

Quotas and monitoring efforts described in Alternative 1 would not be in place since only Tundra swans would be authorized to be taken. Some general monitoring of the hunt would be conducted but not for purposes of quota management. Law enforcement efforts would continue as part of the Tundra swan season with protection for Trumpeters accomplished through education, deterrence and, if necessary, apprehension of individuals who illegally harvest a Trumpeter.

C.   ALTERNATIVE 3 - CLOSE TUNDRA SWAN HUNTING IN TRUMPETER HABITAT:

Under Alternative 3, the Service would close areas to Tundra swan hunting in those parts of Montana, Utah, and/or Nevada that are likely to be used by Trumpeter swans.

Permits issued would depend on areas that remained open and would likely be further reduced, if any Tundra swan hunting was permitted. Under this alternative, based on existing information, the Service would close both Montana and Utah to all swan hunting, and also consider further restrictions in Nevada. However, the Service would consider proposals from the affected States for times and places where the States could document that they could still conduct Tundra swan hunts with a negligible risk of harvesting Trumpeter swans. Season framework dates, if offered, would be timed to avoid any take of Trumpeter swans.

Quotas and monitoring efforts described in Alternative 1 would not be in place since only Tundra swans would be authorized to be taken. Some general monitoring of the hunt would be conducted but not for purposes of quota management. Law enforcement efforts would continue as part of the Tundra swan season with protection for Trumpeters accomplished through education, deterrence and, if necessary, apprehension of individuals who illegally harvest a Trumpeter.

SUMMARY OF DIFFERENCES AMONG ALTERNATIVES			
EFFECTS	Alt. 1. Maintain Restructured Swan Hunting Season	Alt. 2. No Action	Alt. 3. Close Swan Hunting in Trumpeter Habitat
Swan Species Allowed in Harvest	All swan species, but not more than 15 may be Trumpeter swans in Nevada (5) and Utah (10).	Tundra swans.	If season is allowed, only Tundra swans.
Hunter Liability for Shooting a Trumpeter Swan	None.	Would be subject to prosecution for illegal take of a species for which there is no open season.	Would be subject to prosecution for illegal take of a species for which there is no open season.
Earliest Season Opening Date	Saturday closest to October 1, which ranges between September 27 and October 3.	Saturday closest to October 1, which ranges between September 27 and October 3.	If season is allowed, date would be modified to prevent potential take of Trumpeter swans.

Latest Season Closing Date	MT -December 1. UT -2nd Sunday in December, which ranges between December 8-14. NV -1st Sunday following January 1(January 2-8).	Sunday closest to January 20, which ranges between January 17-23.	If season is allowed, date would be modified to prevent potential take of Trumpeter swans.
Season Length in Days	Maximum allowed within outside framework dates but less than 100 days.	100 days.	If season is allowed, length would be determined by outside dates but would be less than 100 days.
Trumpeter Swan Quota and Season Closure	Quota not required in Montana. 15 Trumpeters to be allocated between Utah and Nevada, with season closure should quota be attained.	No quota. No authorized season on Trumpeter swans.	No quota. No authorized season on Trumpeter swans.
Winter Range Distribution	Active participation by the Service. Participation by Pacific Flyway States dependent on interest, status of swan populations, and whether conflicts with hunt programs would be minimal or mitigated.	Active participation by the Service. Participation by states without swan hunts dependent on interest and status of swan populations. Other states may be reluctant to participate because of potential conflicts with hunt programs.	Active participation by the Service. Participation by States without swan hunts dependent on interest and status of swan populations. Support in other States may vary depending on perception of long-term impacts on harvest opportunities and habitat constraints.
Harvest Information	All hunters are required to report harvest and effort information via mail survey. Species composition would be by post-card bill measurement reporting in Montana and examination of all or part of bird by biologists in Utah and Nevada.	All hunters are required to report harvest and effort information via mail survey. Law enforcement efforts would continue as part of the Tundra swan season with protection for Trumpeters accomplished through apprehension of individuals who illegally harvest a Trumpeter.	If season is allowed, all hunters are required to report harvest and effort information via mail survey. Law enforcement efforts would continue as part of the Tundra swan season with protection for Trumpeters accomplished through apprehension of individuals who illegally harvest a Trumpeter.

III.   DESCRIPTION OF THE AFFECTED ENVIRONMENT

A.   THE SWAN BASE

Three swan species are native to North America: Tundra, Trumpeter, and whooper swans (*C. cygnus*). Except as vagrants, whooper swans occur only during winter and then mainly in the western Aleutian Islands; and they would be unaffected by this action. Ranges of the Trumpeter (Fig. 1) and Tundra swans (Fig. 2) include extensive areas throughout Canada and the United States. A fourth species, the mute swan, was introduced from Europe and feral populations are present throughout parts of northern North America and would potentially be affected by this action.

1.   Trumpeter Swans

Trumpeter swans are segregated for management purposes, not biological differences, into three populations: (1) the RMP, focus of this proposal, consists of a migratory flock from interior Canada, a largely sedentary flock from the Tristate area (portions of Montana, Idaho, and Wyoming), both of which winter primarily in the Tristate area, and restoration flocks elsewhere in Wyoming, Idaho, Oregon, Nevada (Fig. 1); (2) the Pacific Coast Population, which breeds mainly in Alaska and winters along the northern Pacific Coast (Fig. 1); and (3) the Interior Population, which is an amalgamation of independent restoration efforts in South Dakota, Nebraska, Minnesota, Michigan, Wisconsin, Iowa, Ontario, Ohio, and New York (Fig. 1).

Terminology related to various geographic components of the RMP of Trumpeter swans has been a source of confusion to many agencies and individuals who have expressed an interest in the stewardship of this population. Over the years the geographic components of the RMP have been called segments, subpopulations, populations, and flocks. There is little biological information upon which to decide if one term is more appropriate than the other. For clarity and consistency the Service has adopted the terminology from the 1998 Pacific Flyway Management Plan (Pacific Flyway Council 1998) and this terminology is used throughout this Environmental Assessment:

> The "Tristate Area" refers to southeast Idaho, southwest Montana, and northwest Wyoming. The "Core Tristate Area" refers to Harriman State Park (HSP), Island Park Reservoir, Teton Basin, Henry's and South Forks of the Snake River and Camas NWR of Idaho; Red Rocks Lakes National Wildlife Refuge (RRLNWR), Centennial Valley, Hebgen Lake and Madison River and tributaries of Montana, and Yellowstone National Park and Jackson Hole of Wyoming (Fig. 3). The "Tristate Region" refers to the entire States of Idaho, Montana, and Wyoming. RMP Trumpeter swans that summer in the U.S. are referred to as the "RMP/U.S. Flocks". "Tristate Flocks" refers specifically to swans that summer in the "Core Tristate Area". "RMP/Canadian flocks" refers to Trumpeters that summer in Canada and winter in the United States.

Trumpeter swan numbers are estimated by a number of surveys throughout North America. The population index most relied upon by managers is the coordinated summer survey instituted in 1968 and conducted at 5-year intervals since 1975 (Caithamer 2001).
The most recent survey was conducted in 2000. Based upon seven continental surveys during 1968-2000, Trumpeter swans have increased at about 6 percent per year over the survey period and now total more than 23,000 birds as of the late-summer of 2000. This total represents an increase of about 535% between the 1968 survey and the most recent survey in 2000. More than 1,000 additional Trumpeters are now in captivity and being held by aviculturists and zoos. All three management populations have been growing at approximately the same rates since these surveys were instituted. The RMP, as a whole, is exhibiting exponential growth over the time span covered by these surveys and totaled more than 3,600 in 2000 (Caithamer 2001, Fig. 4). This number

represents an increase of more than 350% since 1968 and 45% since the 1995 survey. It should be noted that the 1995 survey was conducted prior to the implementation of the experimental swan regulations allowing the limited take of Trumpeter swans in the Pacific Flyway. The 2000 survey represents the population status at the end of the first 5-year experimental hunt period.

RMP Trumpeter swans are also surveyed annually during the winter (Olson 2001), and the U.S. portion of the RMP is also inventoried annually in the fall, prior to the arrival of Canadian migrants (Reed 2000). Based upon winter counts during February, 2001, RMP Trumpeter swans numbered 3,975 (Olson 2001). This figure supports the conclusion of continued population growth and is in reasonably close agreement with the results of the 2000 range-wide survey (Caithamer 2001). Based on the midwinter survey for the period 1972-2001, the RMP continues to increase at about 6 percent each year and averages about 20 percent young in the winter population.

As indicated above, managers recognize that the RMP of Trumpeter swans originates from a variety of breeding areas, as is true of most migratory bird populations in North America. These areas are sometimes divided into groups: those that nest in Canada; those that nest in the Tristate region of Montana, Wyoming, and Idaho; and those that have been established through expansion efforts in Wyoming, Montana, Idaho, Utah, Nevada, and Oregon (see previous section on terminology). Trends in the population indices for these three groups, as measured by winter counts that are not precise in apportioning flock composition, have not been consistent. Similarly, management activities undertaken in recent years apparently have not had the same impact on all components of this population. Numbers of RMP Trumpeter swans breeding in Canada have continued to increase steadily, while numbers of Trumpeter swans breeding in the United States declined substantially following the cessation of the winter feeding program at RRLNWR and associated management actions in the winter of 1992/93. These actions predated the time when harvest of both swan species was permitted in the Pacific Flyway. Since that time, swan numbers in the conterminous United States have been recovering, although they have not reached levels present during the active winter feeding program (Fig. 4).

In summary, since 1995, numbers of RMP Trumpeter swans have continued to increase substantially, despite the authorization of a limited take associated with the existing Tundra swan seasons beginning in that year. Numbers of RMP Trumpeter swans breeding within the United States have only partially recovered from the recent low number estimated in 1993. They have not reached levels that were present in the United States before the cessation of feeding programs at RRLNWR and the institution of other intensive management activities that were undertaken to address the winter distribution concerns of this population.

Trumpeters are classified as a migratory game bird. Prior to 1995, Trumpeter swans had not been hunted, since Federal protection was authorized first in 1913 and then successfully in 1918. They are not classified as being either "threatened" or "endangered" under the Endangered Species Act; although, in the 1960s, the species was listed under the Service's "Red Book" based on the limited understanding of it's status at that time. The Red Book is an international compilation of globally threatened or endangered species prepared under the auspices of the International Union for the Conservation of Nature. In 1989, the Service was petitioned to list the RMP as threatened, but the petition presented information insufficient to conclude that such listing was warranted (55(81)Federal Register: 17646-17648, April 16, 1990).

On August 22, 2000 the Service was petitioned to list a portion of the RMP of Trumpeter swans. The petitioners requested that the Service consider emergency listing of the Tristate flock. The Service acknowledged receipt of the petition and informed the petitioners that listing funds are not currently available for processing of administrative petition findings. Additionally, the Service stated that the population trend data for the RMP swans indicated that there was no compelling evidence to indicate that emergency listing was appropriate. On February 5, 2001, the petitioners provided a 60-day notice of intent to sue over our failure to prepare a 90-day finding on the petition. The Service responded to this notice on April 5, 2001, and indicated that all listing funds for FY 2001 have already been allocated to court settlements and court ordered deadlines, so it will not be possible to prepare any additional administrative petition findings. Additionally, the Service stated that the population trend data for RMP Trumpeter swans indicated that there was no compelling evidence to show that emergency listing was appropriate and further noted that the portion of the RMP recommended for listing in the petition has also been stable to increasing since the winter of 1992-1993.

The winter distribution of Trumpeter swans in the Pacific Flyway remains concentrated primarily in Southeastern Idaho and the potential for winter losses continues. Heavy wintering use is made of the Henry's Fork of the Snake River by RMP Trumpeter swans, causing significant damage to habitat of a world-class trout fishery. Perhaps, more than a hundred swans died from starvation on the Henry's Fork in the winter of 1988-89, although exact numbers are not known. The die-off drew considerable media attention and prompted the 1989-petitioning for Endangered Species Act listing. However, since 1989 there have been few winter losses recorded and the hazing program has helped limit further growth of this wintering concentration in this specific area. During the winter of 2000-2001, numbers of Trumpeter swans associated with HSP totaled only about 20 percent of the total midwinter population. The Service notes that waterfowl distributions and migratory behavior are often impacted by weather events. Migratory birds are among the most resilient groups of animals in their ability to react to such changing conditions. The Service fully expects that variable weather conditions (such as freezing conditions or drought) will be encountered in the future and believes such natural occurrences should be considered as part of the birds natural environment and, as such, weather events should not precipitate management actions unless or until evidence of significant direct mortality can be demonstrated. Should weather events lead to an appreciable movement of Trumpeter swans into existing hunt zones, the Service believes that the quota system in place will preclude any population level effects.

The Pacific Flyway Management Plan for RMP Trumpeter Swans (Subcommittee on RMP Trumpeter Swans 1998), endorsed by the Pacific Flyway Council and supported by the Service, calls for aggressive action to broaden the breeding and winter distribution of swans and restore a tradition for migration, in part, to alleviate chronic wintering problems. Since 1990, the Service, States, Bureau of Reclamation, and others have spent more than $1 million in trapping, translocating, hazing, and monitoring activities. Efforts to re-establish migratory behavior have shown limited success to date.

2.   Tundra Swans:

Tundra swans are segregated for management purposes into two populations: (1) the WP, object of this proposal, which breeds in western Alaska, migrates mainly through the Tristate area, Utah, and Nevada, as well as along the west coast, to winter mainly in California (Fig. 2); and (2) the Eastern Population (EP), which breeds mainly in Arctic Canada and winters mainly on the eastern U.S. coast.

Numbers of Tundra swans are indexed annually by the midwinter survey conducted in major waterfowl concentration areas across North America. Indices for both Eastern and Western Populations display long-term upward trends. The WP has increased at an annual rate of about two-percent per year since 1955, reaching record high numbers during the last 4 years. The most recent midwinter index suggested about 90,000 Tundra swans in the WP in January of 2001 (Fig. 5).

The Pacific Flyway Council and the Service cooperatively developed management plans for WP Tundra swans (Subcommittee on Whistling Swans 1983). Objectives include:

- Maintain a 3-year average population index of at least 38,000 swans as estimated by the midwinter waterfowl survey;

- Maintain current patterns of distribution throughout the swan's range;

- Provide breeding, migration, and wintering habitats of sufficient quantity and quality to maintain the desired numbers and distribution of swans; and

- Provide for aesthetic, educational, scientific, and hunting uses of these swans.

A companion hunt plan for WP Tundra swans (Pacific Flyway Study Committee 1989) developed a strategy that would allow for an annual harvest commensurate with maintaining a long-term winter population of at least 38,000 birds. The hunt plan also recognized that in order to protect Trumpeter swans zone closures and season modifications to Tundra swan seasons should be considered.

Federally authorized hunting seasons on Tundra swans were first allowed in Utah in 1962. WP Tundra swan seasons are now allowed in portions of Alaska, Montana, Utah, and Nevada. Seasons on EP Tundra swans are authorized for Montana (Central Flyway portion), North Dakota, South Dakota, Virginia, North Carolina, and New Jersey. Sport hunting programs are endorsed by all Flyway Councils with a harvest objective of generally less than 10 percent of the winter population. Harvest is allocated among States by permits. State-administered permit systems provide good estimates of harvest. Sport harvest of the WP and EP is less than 2 and 4 percent of their respective midwinter swan population indices; but the combined subsistence harvest (8 percent) and sport harvest (2 percent) of the WP total about 10 percent. Trost et al. (2000) provide a summary of permit allocation, hunter participation, harvest, and age-composition of the harvest, by State, as related to WP Tundra swans (Tables 1a-1d).

3.   Mute Swans:

Mute swans became established in North America through escapes and intentional releases from captivity. In the Atlantic and Mississippi Flyways where they breed in the wild, more than 7,000 birds on average were counted during winter surveys in 1985-94. In the Pacific Flyway, feral mute swans were first recorded in the midwinter inventory in 1975, averaged 3 swans per year during 1975-95, ranging upwards to 14 individuals. The Pacific Flyway distribution of mute swans in the wild is largely dependent upon where they escaped or were released from captivity, with most being reported in Washington and Oregon; however, they were reported in Nevada and California during 2 winters. Mute swans are not among those species protected by the Migratory Bird Treaty Act of 1918 (see "List of Migratory Birds" at 50 CFR 10.13) and are considered an invasive exotic species in some portions of their range, e.g., Chesapeake Bay of Maryland and Virginia.

B. THE SWAN HABITATS

1. Trumpeter Swans:

Trumpeter swans historically occurred over much of northern North America, excluding arctic areas, with populations wintering along the Atlantic, Pacific, and Gulf of Mexico coasts. Trumpeters nested in the prairies and bottomlands of the mid-continent where they were among the first waterfowl to be negatively impacted by settlement. Today, RMP Trumpeters nest in small wetlands and lakes in subarctic taiga, boreal forest, and aspen parklands in southern Yukon, northeastern British Columbia, southern Mackenzie District, Alberta, and southeastern Saskatchewan. In addition to the Canadian nesting areas, RMP Trumpeter swans nest in lakes and other wetlands in the mountainous portions of the Tristate area of Montana, Idaho, and Wyoming, and in some of the Great Basin marshes found in Nevada and Oregon generally seeking undisturbed habitats with aquatic foods. The Centennial Valley, Teton Basin, Yellowstone Park, Harney Basin, Summer Lake, and Ruby Lake are some of the more important Trumpeter nesting areas in the western United States for the RMP of Trumpeter swans.

Aside from restoration flocks in Oregon and Nevada, which are largely non-migratory and primarily of Tristate origin, a majority of RMP Trumpeter swans stage in fall or winter in the Tristate area. This large concentration of migrating and wintering RMP Trumpeter swans in and near HSP on the Henry's Fork of the Snake River in southeastern Idaho and at RRLNWR in southwestern Montana is the chief management concern for this population. Swans and other waterfowl using the HSP sanctuary have, in some winters, so depleted the submerged aquatic vegetation that they are at risk of starvation. Starvation losses and poor nutrition prior to onset of nesting may limit prospects for Trumpeter swan population growth and range expansion, however, this does not appear to have occurred as yet.

Translocated swans use sites in the American Falls Reservoir in southeastern Idaho. Migrant swans from the Canadian flock have been observed as far south as the Central Valley of California; and they likely arrived there after following Tundra swan migration corridors through Montana, Idaho, Utah, and Nevada. In general, wintering swans are dependent on naturally-occurring aquatic plants in sufficient abundance and nutritional quality. They have not yet adapted to feeding in agricultural fields as have many other species of waterfowl.

2. Tundra Swans:

WP Tundra swans breed in western Alaska and, as their name implies, in tundra habitat. They are found during summer from the Koyukuk River south to the Alaska Peninsula. Some birds nest on Kodiak Island, but the vast majority occur on the Yukon-Kuskokwim Delta (Fig. 2). In migration, WP swans follow both coastal (minor) and interior (major) routes and use a diversity of habitat types ranging from estuarine, fresh-water, alkaline, natural, agricultural and wildlife-managed sites. Tundra swans rely extensively upon aquatic vegetation throughout the year. In migration and wintering areas, sago pondweed is a favored food plant, but they will frequent upland areas to graze on grasses, sedges, and berries. They have learned to glean grain from both dry and flooded agricultural fields and forage on pasture to supplement their natural aquatic diet.

3.   Mute Swans:

Mute swans occupy the same habitats used by other swans and waterfowl and potentially compete with them for food and space.

C.   AFFECTED AND INTERESTED PARTIES

The proposed action predominately and directly affects residents of Montana, Utah, and Nevada. People living elsewhere, but having an active interest and/or direct involvement in management of swans may also be affected.

1.   RECREATIONAL HUNTERS

The proposed action would directly affect the approximately 5,400 hunters who applied for the 3,150 total permits available in Utah (2,000), Montana (500), and Nevada (650) for the 2000-2001 hunting season. This number is also approximately the long-term average number of hunters who have applied for swan hunting permits in these States.

2.   NON-GOVERNMENTAL ORGANIZATIONS AND THE PUBLIC

The proposed action predominately and directly affects residents of Montana, Utah, and Nevada. People living elsewhere but having an active interest and/or direct involvement in management of swans may also be affected.   The proposed action would directly affect NGOs actively involved with Trumpeter swan restoration, specifically The Trumpeter Swan Society (approaching 500 members in 1995) which promotes the well being and restoration of Trumpeter swans, and the Henry's Fork Foundation (700 members) which promotes dispersal of Trumpeter swans and other waterfowl on the Henry's Fork River in order to restore the damaged world-class trout fisheries. Additional NGOs that have expressed an interest in this issue include the Humane Society of the United States, The Fund for Animals, Inc., the Animal Protection Institute, and the Biodiversity Legal Foundation. Many members of the general public have also directly contacted Service representatives concerning this issue.

1.   BUSINESS

The proposed action would affect businesses that are partially dependent upon meeting the needs of hunters and services associated with trumpeter swan restoration efforts.

IV.   ENVIRONMENTAL CONSEQUENCES

This section is comprised of a summary of the environmental consequences of implementing each of the alternatives on swan populations, their habitat, recreational activities and other factors identified during preparation and review of previous Environmental Assessments on this issue. A summary of these issues and the Service response is provided in previous Service documents on this issue (Draft EA, Appendix B). The assessment and analysis included in Appendix B was prepared to summarize our evaluation of implementing the various alternatives and was used extensively in preparing this section. Most recent comments received have been very similar to these previous comments and much of this previous discussion is reiterated in the Summary of comments included here. A summary of impacts is also presented in Table form at the end of this section.

A. ALTERNATIVE 1 (PREFERRED ALTERNATIVE) - ALLOW A LIMITED TAKE OF TRUMPETER SWANS DURING GENERAL SWAN HUNTING SEASONS:

The proposed action would authorize a small take of trumpeter swans during established tundra swan seasons in designated portions of Montana, Utah and Nevada, within the Pacific Flyway provided that quotas are not exceeded for Trumpeter Swans. Possession, transportation, and disposition of all swan species would be governed by regulations applicable to all other waterfowl species (see 50 CFR Part 20).

The Tundra swan hunting season that existed prior to 1995 was significantly modified by both the 1995 and the 2000 Environmental Assessments and subsequent regulations on this issue. This proposal would maintain all of these alterations, specifically the area restrictions that were then imposed, the number of permits to be allocated in Montana, Utah and Nevada, and the harvest monitoring requirements.

The area restrictions were imposed to afford greater protection to Trumpeter swans and the earlier season closure dates were also implemented with the idea that if Trumpeter swans were moving in the Pacific Flyway, they would be more likely be moving later in the season and an earlier closure would afford additional protection to any dispersing Trumpeter swans.

In addition to season area, permit and time modifications, the Service will expand it's role in cooperative efforts to enhance the breeding and wintering distribution of Trumpeter swans throughout the Pacific Flyway under this alternative. The Service will seek concurrence of State, other Federal Agency and NGO partners by requesting participation in the development of a detailed implementation plan to achieve the goals and objectives of the Pacific Flyway's 1998 RMP Trumpeter Swan Management Plan. The Service will attempt to achieve this action through introduction of additional Trumpeter swans into suitable habitat throughout the Pacific Flyway, and by continuing management efforts to discourage use of the Tristate wintering concentration area.

a. THE SWAN BASE

Trumpeter Swan: The Service would: (1) actively participate in efforts to enhance the breeding and winter distribution of Trumpeter swans, and (2) maintain the biologically acceptable, but conservative harvest quota of 15 Trumpeter swans in Utah and Nevada. The Service notes that during the past six years, RMP Trumpeter swans exhibited a substantial population increase as measured by both the 5-year periodic survey and the annual midwinter estimates (Caithamer 2001, Olson 2001). This population increase occurred during the period when the legal take of Trumpeter swans was permitted. This increase occurred despite losses to the population caused by direct management activities (i.e. the translocation program). Further, the increase was seen in both the US and Canadian flocks (Caithamer 2001). The Service recognizes that not all components of the population appear to be increasing at the same rate, however, as noted in the status review, increases in the Tristate area are not expected to equal those in the more northern areas because of existing habitat limitations. The Service believes that the six years of experience with the limited Trumpeter swan hunting option clearly demonstrates that neither the population nor any geographic component of the population is likely to be adversely impacted following implementation of this alternative. Under the provisions of this alternative the take of one Trumpeter Swan was documented in the previous hunting season in Utah and none were known to have been taken in Nevada. Anticipated take in future seasons is therefore expected to be very low.

Tundra Swan: The number and distribution of Tundra swans in Montana, Utah and Nevada has been largely unaffected by previous implementation of the actions contained in this alternative. The number of permits authorizing the take of swans would be maintained at the levels established in the 2000-2001 hunting season for Montana, Nevada and Utah. The anticipated harvest of Tundra swans would remain within harvest management guidelines for the population. Tundra swan populations are currently above population objective levels.

Mute Swan: The number and distribution of mute swans would be largely unaffected by this action since very few birds occur in Utah, Montana or Nevada. The species would remain unprotected by the Migratory Bird Treaty Act of 1918, as amended.

b.   THE SWAN HABITATS

Hazing, elimination of supplemental feeding, and other cooperative efforts to make current wintering habitats less hospitable (such as attempting to maintain high flow rates in the Henry's Fork) would continue. Due to concerns and doubts about the effectiveness of translocations, the Service will only support this activity on a limited, case by case basis and not as the preferred means of addressing the winter distribution problem. Further, the Service will request State, NGO, and other Federal agency cooperators to join in development of a detailed implementation plan to achieve the goals and objectives of the 1998 Flyway Management Plan. This plan should contain guidelines for translocation activities for use in the Pacific Flyway. The Service has completed a draft of it's portion of the implementation plan with suggestions for activities on National Wildlife Refuges within RMP range (Appendix A). In summary, implementation of the portions of Alternative 2 dealing with swan harvest are not expected to have a significant affect on the habitats used by Trumpeter, Tundra or Mute swans.

c.   RECREATIONAL HUNTING IMPACTS

In Montana, hunters will not be able to hunt swans in the western portions of Pondera & Teton Counties (areas formally open to Tundra swan hunting). However, the new opportunities afforded those hunting in the larger Chouteau County that were instituted in 1995 will be maintained.

The Nevada swan season will be closed upon attainment of their assigned quota (established at 5 Trumpeter swans). Areas open to hunting in Nevada and season dates will remain unchanged from those established in the 1995 Environmental Assessment.

In Utah, the additional constraints placed on swan hunting opportunities in the 2000-2001 hunting season would be continued. These constraints reduced the number of permits issued from 2,750 to 2,000; reduced the quota on Trumpeter swan take from 15 to 10; and reduced the area open to swan hunting by the closure of all areas north of the northern boundary of the BRMBR to all swan hunting.

a.   AESTHETIC IMPACTS

Under this alternative Persons and NGOs interested in viewing swans will be impacted during the period of the swan season due to curtailed viewing opportunities. This will be for a relatively short period of time and opportunities for swan viewing will still be available in some locations. The additional restrictions on hunting opportunity implemented in the 1999-2000 season would provide greater opportunity for viewing swans. In summary, impacts will be short term and the number of Trumpeters harvested is expected to be low causing minimal impact on viewing opportunity. The number of Tundra swans authorized to be taken is also low and would probably not be noticeable in terms of viewing opportunity or other aesthetic concerns.

NGOs and persons either opposed to swan hunting or interested in an expedited winter-range expansion effort for Trumpeter swans would continue to be dissatisfied with the Tundra swan seasons because of the potential loss of pioneering Trumpeter swans.

b.   LOCAL ECONOMIC IMPACTS

Business would continue to provide equipment and services to hunters and agencies involved in swan restoration efforts. Otherwise, impacts on the local economy are expected to be minimal.

2.   ALTERNATIVE 2 - NO ACTION:

Under the "No Action" alternative, the *status quo*, i.e., frameworks for seasons that were in effect during 1988-93, would be maintained. Areas, seasons and numbers of permits for Tundra swan hunting in Montana, Utah, and Idaho, would be unmodified from those in place between 1983 and 1994. The entire State of Utah would be open to Tundra swan hunting. The Service would continue to establish open seasons on Tundra swans in parts of Montana and Nevada and throughout Utah while maintaining a "closed season" on Trumpeter swans. Seasons could continue through the Sunday closest to January 20 and not exceed 100 days.

a.   THE SWAN BASE

Trumpeter Swan: The Service would continue to participate in cooperative efforts to improve winter-range distribution of Trumpeter swans within parts of the Pacific Flyway as described in Alternative 1. Should Trumpeter swans enter Tundra swan hunt areas, because of hazing or through pioneering, they would not be afforded additional protection associated with time or area restrictions on hunting opportunity. Those swans arriving in late winter would therefore experience an increased risk of being killed during a Tundra swan season. Such an unregulated harvest could possibly slow the rate of pioneering and winter range distribution if enough Trumpeters were taken. The overall Trumpeter swan population would continue to increase but at a slower rate.

Impacts on Trumpeter swans would be potentially the highest among all alternatives and it would be difficult to track population impacts absent a monitoring program.

Tundra Swan: The number and distribution of Tundra swans would be largely unaffected by this action with impacts anticipated to be similar to that described under Alternative 1.

Mute Swan: The number and distribution of mute swans would be largely unaffected by this action since very few birds occur in Utah, Montana or Nevada. The species would remain unprotected by the Migratory Bird Treaty Act of 1918, as amended.

b.   THE SWAN HABITATS

Hazing, elimination of supplemental feeding, and other cooperative efforts to make current wintering habitats less hospitable (such as attempting to maintain high flow rates in the Henry's Fork) would continue. Due to concerns and doubts about the effectiveness of translocations, the Service will only support this activity on a limited, case by case basis and not as the preferred means of addressing the winter distribution problem. Further, the Service will request State, NGO, and other Federal agency cooperators to join in development of a detailed implementation plan to achieve the goals and objectives of the 1998 Flyway Management Plan. This plan should contain guidelines for translocation activities for use in the Pacific Flyway. The Service has completed a draft of it's portion of the implementation plan with suggestions for activities on National Wildlife Refuges within RMP range (Appendix A).   In summary, implementation of the portions of Alternative 2 dealing with swan harvest are not expected to have a significant affect on the habitats used by Trumpeter, Tundra or Mute swans.

c.   RECREATIONAL HUNTING IMPACTS

Not more than 500, 2,500, and 650 permittee's in Montana, Utah, and Nevada, respectively, would still be able to hunt. In Utah, the State-wide hunt would result in some hunting activity in places where swans are significantly less abundant, both spatially and temporally, than in the Great Salt Lake Basin.

The Service and State agencies could issue citations and prosecute Tundra swan hunters who accidentally took Trumpeter swans during an open season on Tundra swans.

Hunters would have a significant disincentive to comply with harvest surveys requirements as detection of a Trumpeter swan by such methods would make them liable to prosecution.

a.   AESTHETIC IMPACTS

Under this alternative Persons and NGOs interested in viewing swans will be impacted during the period of the swan season due to curtailed viewing opportunities. This will be for a relatively short period of time and opportunities for swan viewing will still be available in some locations. Areas potentially impacted would be greater than that described under Alternative 1 since there would be no specific area closures in habitats with significant Trumpeter swan use. In summary, impacts will be short term and, although the number of Trumpeters harvested may increase, impacts on viewing opportunity are expected to be low. The number of Tundra swans authorized to be taken is also low and would probably not be noticeable in terms of viewing opportunity or other aesthetic concerns.

NGOs and persons either opposed to swan hunting or interested in an expedited winter-range expansion effort for Trumpeter swans would continue to be dissatisfied with the Tundra swan seasons because of the potential loss of pioneering Trumpeter swans.

Swans would continue to be discouraged from using wintering sites with limited food resources by hazing, and they would not be fed. Additionally, States may be reluctant to accept wintering swans because of uncertainties related to ongoing waterfowl seasons.

b.   LOCAL ECONOMIC IMPACTS

Businesses would continue to provide equipment and services to hunters and agencies involved in swan restoration efforts.

3.   ALTERNATIVE 3 - SEVERELY RESTRICT OR CLOSE TUNDRA SWAN HUNTING:

Under Alternative 3 the Service would either severely restrict or not allow open seasons on Tundra swans in those parts of Montana, Utah, or Nevada that are likely to be used by Trumpeter swans. This may occur in situations where range expansion efforts prove successful, or where there is recent information on the occurrence of Trumpeter swans. Seasons, if allowed, would be structured specifically to prevent any incidental take of Trumpeters swans during Tundra swan seasons. Depending on current and future swan distribution this could lead to a situation where waterfowl hunting could be similar to that experienced by hunters in Utah prior to 1962, in Nevada prior to 1969, and in Montana prior to 1970, when waterfowl seasons were closed to the taking of any swan species.

a.   THE SWAN BASE

Trumpeter Swan: The Service would continue to participate in cooperative efforts to improve winter-range distribution of Trumpeter swans within parts of the Pacific Flyway. The risk of Trumpeter swans being shot during a general waterfowl season would be significantly reduced because there likely would be no open season in Tundra swan concentration areas which are also the areas likely to be used by Trumpeter swans. Overall, the Trumpeter swan population would likely increase at a slightly greater rate and perhaps become more widely distributed in winter than under Alternatives 1 or 2. Nevertheless, the Service does not believe that curtailing or eliminating hunting opportunity will result in a significant increase in population status or distribution. This is largely due to the very low number of Trumpeter swans that have been harvested historically and the rapidly increasing population trends which have been documented during the previous experimental period.

Tundra Swan: The number and distribution of Tundra swans would be largely unaffected by this action. Relative to the overall population status and trends of the WP of Tundra swans only minor impacts on the population are anticipated. Some minor increase in numbers may occur since hunting opportunity would be reduced to eliminate impacts on Trumpeter swans.

Mute Swan: The number and distribution of mute swans would be largely unaffected by this action since very few birds occur in Utah, Montana or Nevada. The species would remain unprotected by the Migratory Bird Treaty Act of 1918, as amended.

b.   THE SWAN HABITATS

Hazing, elimination of supplemental feeding, and other cooperative efforts to make current wintering habitats less hospitable (such as attempting to maintain high flow rates in the Henry's Fork) would continue. Due to concerns and doubts about the effectiveness of translocations, the Service will only support this activity on a limited, case by case basis and not as the preferred means of addressing the winter distribution problem. Further, the Service will request State, NGO, and other Federal agency cooperators to join in development of a detailed implementation plan to achieve the goals and objectives of the 1998 Flyway Management Plan. This plan should contain guidelines for translocation activities for use in the Pacific Flyway. The Service has completed a draft of it's portion of the implementation plan with suggestions for activities on National Wildlife Refuges within RMP range (Appendix A).

Hazing Trumpeter swans from crowded wintering sites on the Henry's Fork of the Snake River has potential to allow habitats to recover from recent, excessive use by waterfowl. However, potentially increasing numbers of Tundra swans could in some localities compete with Trumpeter swans for winter-limited resources.

In summary, implementation of the portions of any Alternative dealing with swan harvest are not expected to have a significant affect on the habitats used by Trumpeter, Tundra or Mute swans.

c.   RECREATIONAL HUNTING IMPACTS

If swan hunting was not allowed, it is expected that some swans would occasionally be illegally taken concurrent with waterfowl seasons. When detected, violators would be issued citations, prosecuted, and the dead swans confiscated. Due to difficulty in determining the difference between Tundra and Trumpeter swans and the need to close areas used by Trumpeter swans recreational hunting opportunity would be greatly curtailed. Potentially, 3,650 hunters would be denied an opportunity to hunt swans.

d.   AESTHETIC IMPACTS

This alternative would provide the greatest benefit to NGOs and persons opposed to swan hunting and NGOs supportive of Trumpeter swan restoration efforts. Swan viewing opportunities would be enhanced since many areas used by swans would be closed to hunting.

In Idaho and Montana hazing swans from over-crowded wintering sites would be continued as would the suspension of artificial feeding. Should the hazing program result in displacement of some swans to neighboring states there would likely be some reluctance to accept hazed swans because of the impact of the program on traditional hunting opportunities.

e. LOCAL ECONOMIC IMPACTS

Business partially dependent upon swan hunters would have diminished sales. Some benefit might be derived from enhanced opportunities to view swans.

SUMMARY OF EFFECTS AMONG ALTERNATIVES			
EFFECTS	Alt. 1. Restructured Swan Hunting Season	Alt. 2. No Action	Alt. 3. Severely Restrict or Close Swan Hunting
Winter Distribution of Trumpeter Swans	Risk to Trumpeter swans potentially moving along Tundra swan migration corridors in the Pacific Flyway would be controlled. Protection for Trumpeters would be enhanced due to early season closures and expanded area closures in Utah.	Trumpeter swans will expand their winter range, but those moving into hunt areas in late winter would be at potential risk from up to 100-day swan seasons.	Trumpeters following Tundra swan migration corridors would be at minimal risk from waterfowl hunting.
Trumpeter Swan Status	Trumpeter swans would be legally taken but their number limited and monitored. Tristate group of swans would likely increase due to augmentation. They would remain subject to a die-off in SE Idaho but with less impact on the population. The Canadian group would continue to increase.	Trumpeter swans would be shot accidentally during Tundra swan seasons but the take mostly not monitored. Tristate group of swans would remain stable or decrease, and would be subject to a die-off in SE Idaho. The Canadian group would continue to increase.	The Tristate group of swans would remain stable or increase, but would be subject to a die-off in SE Idaho. The Canadian group would continue to increase.
Tundra Swan Status	Tundra swans would continue to be harvested with the maximum take guided by a Flyway-approved harvest strategy but constrained by safeguards for Trumpeter swans. Tundra swan numbers would likely remain stable or increase should harvest be reduced.	Tundra swans would continue to be harvested with the maximum take guided by a Flyway-approved harvest strategy. Tundra swan numbers would likely remain stable or continue to increase.	If season was allowed, Tundra swans could be taken but likely the total harvest would be reduced. Tundra swan numbers likely would increase at a faster rate unless subsistence harvests were to increase.

Swan Hunting Opportunity & Success	Hunter numbers would be further reduced (3,150). Hunter days could be reduced or remain unchanged should hunters redirect their activities. Hunter success is likely to increase because effort will be concentrated in both time and area where Tundra swans are most abundant. Season potentially would be terminated early by achieving quota of Trumpeter swans.	A maximum of 3,650 permits would be authorized for hunters to hunt potentially 100 days between approximately October 1 and January 20. Montana hunters could hunt in all of Pondera and Teton counties but not Chouteau County. Utah hunters could hunt state-wide.	Hunting opportunity for 3,650 hunters would be curtailed significantly and potentially eliminated depending on swan distribution.
Hunter Liability	Swan hunters taking a Trumpeter swan could do so legally. Season would terminate should quota be obtained preventing additional take. Hunters taking swans following season closure would be subject to prosecution.	Swan hunters taking Trumpeter swans would be subject to prosecution.	Should a season be allowed, swan hunters taking Trumpeter swans would be subject to prosecution.
Public Attitudes	Hunters would be displeased with restrictions. Most NGOs and the public who do not support a balanced approach to either hunting or restoration would be displeased.	Hunters would be pleased with minimal restrictions and inconvenience but risk prosecution. Various NGOs would be dissatisfied with progress at enhancing Trumpeter swan redistr bution.	Hunters would be displeased. Various NGOs would be satisfied that progress was being made to enhance Trumpeter swan redistribution; but some of those would be dissatisfied that it was done at the expense of hunting.
Costs to Hunters to Administer Programs	Potential added costs in fees to administer a more restricted program. Hunters may need to travel further to hunt; and they will be required submit birds for examination in Utah and Nevada and report via postcard in Montana.	No additional costs in money or time.	If a season allowed, reduced costs and hunting opportunity. If season is closed, no costs and hunting opportunity will be eliminated.

Costs to Agencies to Administer Programs	Additional costs for obtaining hunter and harvest information data and enforcement related to general swan seasons. No additional costs in hazing, translocating, and monitoring Trumpeter swans; but cost-effectiveness of effort potentially greater than Alternative 2 but less than Alternative 3.	Costs of obtaining hunter and harvest information data and enforcement of Tundra swan seasons would continue. Costs to haze, and monitor Trumpeter swans would continue. Cost-effectiveness of effort would be potentially negated by unrestricted take of Trumpeter swans.	Costs related to hunt dependent upon whether or not season is allowed. Costs to haze and monitor Trumpeter swans would continue. Cost-effectiveness of effort potentially will be increased because the accidental take of Trumpeter swans should be minimal.

4. UNAVOIDABLE ADVERSE IMPACTS AND MITIGATIVE MEASURES OF THE ALTERNATIVES

Under Alternative 1 some take of Trumpeter swans would be authorized and such take is likely to occur. Under Alternative 2, some illegal harvest would likely occur in conjunction with Tundra swan hunting because of the difficulties in discrimination between the two species. Under Alternative 1 take of Trumpeters would be monitored and a quota established and enforced to avoid take of more than 15 birds in Utah and Nevada. Mitigative measures such as closure of areas known to have experienced take of Trumpeter swans, reduction in the number of permits and timing of the seasons have been developed to lessen impacts on Trumpeter swans. Implementation of these measures aids growth in the swan population and contributes to a positive working relationship with the various States involved in management by balancing competing needs for hunting and viewing Trumpeters. Continued growth in the Trumpeter swan population throughout it's range and the very low numbers of Trumpeters taken in the past season are evidence that the current management approach is effective. This management scheme when coupled with accelerated efforts to expand the breeding range through reintroduction and habitat management (see Appendix A) is expected to lead to continued growth in RMP Trumpeter swans.

I. SUMMARY OF COMMENTS AND SERVICE CONCLUSIONS

Most comments received fall into two broad general categories; those that believe the Service proposal is too restrictive with regard to proposed hunting seasons under the preferred alternative and those who believe that the Service should prohibit all swan hunting in places where both Tundra and Trumpeter swans may occur or simply prohibit all swan hunting. There were a few comments that were received that did not recommend a specific alternative, but did raise questions or issues that were related to the proposed action. We have provided a response to several of these points as well.

The States of Wyoming, Oregon, Utah, Nevada, Idaho (Department of Fish and Game), the Pacific and Central Flyway Councils, the Conservation Force (on behalf of the Dallas Safari Club, Dallas Ecological Foundation, Houston Safari Club, African Safari Club of Florida, the Louisiana Chapter of the Safari Club International, the National Taxidermist Association, and the Central Louisiana Chapter of Safari Club

International), the Nevada Waterfowl Association and 6 individuals wrote in support of continuation and/or expansion of existing swan hunting opportunities. In contrast, the State of Idaho (Department of Parks and Recreation), The Trumpeter Swan Society (TTSS), The Friends of Animals (FOA), Schubert and Associates (on behalf of the Fund for Animals (FFA), the Humane Society of the United States (HSUS), and the Biodiversity Legal Foundation (BLF)), the Greater Yellowstone Coalition, Public Employees for Environmental Responsibility, the Utah Environmental Congress, the Friends of the West, the Idaho Conservation League, the Salish and Kootenai Tribes, and 143 individuals raised a number of issues that they felt warranted more restrictive, or elimination of, swan hunting opportunities in the Pacific Flyway. Comments were received from Yellowstone National Park, the Bureau of Reclamation, and the Wildlife Management Institute that did not recommend a specific alternative, but did raise several points or issues that were considered by the Service. The following are the Service responses to the specific points raised both in support of additional hunting opportunity and those who recommended either further restrictions or elimination of swan hunting opportunities in the Pacific Flyway and to those who did not recommend a specific alternative.

Comments generally opposed to swan hunting and/or continuation of swan hunting seasons allowing the take of Trumpeter swans.

A number of comments were received that would be categorized as opposed to swan hunting in general, or more specifically opposed to allowing the legal take of Trumpeter swans. These comments are addressed as follows:

As previously stated, the Service supports Tundra swan hunting where and when their population status warrants such activity and Flyway management plans (including harvest management guidelines) have been developed to ensure the long term welfare of these populations. The continued growth of the western population of Tundra swans during the past several decades supports the Service position that harvest and population maintenance and enhancement are not inconsistent. The Service will continue to authorize and support Tundra swan hunting seasons that meet these guidelines.

Many comments referred to Trumpeter swans as either endangered or a threatened species and use this status as the basis for recommending that no harvest of Trumpeter swans be allowed. Trumpeter swans are not, nor have they ever been, listed as either a threatened or endangered species. The three presently recognized populations continue to grow steadily and their geographic range continues to expand under cooperative programs conducted throughout North America to restore this species to it's historic range (Fig. 1). These statements regarding status are not intended to imply that the Service considers Trumpeter swan restoration efforts complete. The Service will continue to actively promote efforts to increase Trumpeter swan numbers throughout North America and to work to establish new migratory Trumpeter swan populations when possible. For example the Service has funded the propagation of approximately 40 cygnets for release in the Tristate area in the near future. The Service would not concur with the position that all harvest of this species should be precluded based on their present population status, but certainly intends to enforce strict limits on the take of Trumpeter swans in Tundra swan seasons to ensure continued growth and expansion of Trumpeter swans. The Service will address the issue of the petition for listing Trumpeter swans nesting within the Tristate area of Montana, Idaho, and Wyoming as a distinct population segment separately below.

As Trumpeter swan restoration efforts continue, additional overlap between the two species in areas open to Tundra swan hunting can reasonably be expected. The Service does not believe that the occasional harvest of a Trumpeter swan in an existing Tundra swan season should preclude such seasons since such harvest would have very little impact on the health or population status of the population. Additionally, the Service does not propose to establish any hunting seasons specifically for Trumpeter swans anywhere in the United States. Rather, the Service will require monitoring that is sufficient to determine specific locations where and when any harvest of Trumpeter swans might occur in Tundra swan seasons, and to adjust Tundra swan seasons, where necessary, to protect Trumpeter swan populations, but not individuals. Although several comments suggest that the burden for protecting Trumpeter swans in Tundra swan seasons should be placed on individual hunters, the Service does not feel such an approach is either reasonable, feasible or necessary. Differentiating Tundra and Trumpeter swans in the field has been described by Patten and Heindel (1994) as "perhaps the most underrated field identification problem in North America". The Service does not feel regulations requiring hunters to make such judgements under field conditions are likely to be effective. However, the Service strongly supports and encourages hunter education efforts to improve hunter identification and to reduce unintentional Trumpeter swan harvest. Likewise, the Service does not believe that hunters should be held liable for the unintentional harvest of a Trumpeter swan. The Service believes that required harvest monitoring programs, establishment of limited quotas on Trumpeter swan harvest and Tundra swan hunting season adjustments can provide sufficient protection to expanding Trumpeter swan populations while maintaining traditional Tundra swan hunting opportunities. As previously stated by the Service, where conflicts arise, the Service will examine and deal with such situations on a case by case basis.

TTSS comments address most of the concerns raised by organizations and individuals who expressed opposition to the implementation of the preferred alternative based on factors other than a general opposition to swan hunting and/or the legal take of Trumpeter swans. The letter submitted in response to the draft EA by TTSS makes 10 statements and then raises some specific points with regard to information presented in the EA. The Service renumbered and combined these comments and offers the following response:

1.   TTSS States: "We strongly support the goal and objectives of the 1998 Pacific Flyway Plan for RMP Trumpeter Swans. However, we are deeply concerned that the Service and Pacific Flyway do not yet have a program in place to achieve those objectives and reduce RMP vulnerability. We are hopeful that the upcoming Implementation Plan process will lead to effective actions and intend to contribute to that effort."

The Service also supports the goals and objectives 1998 Pacific Flyway Management plan. The Service has provided financial, administrative and personnel resources directed at achieving these goals for the past several decades. Additionally, many other Pacific Flyway States and affected government agencies (both Federal and State) have contributed substantially toward achieving these goals. The Service appreciates the contributions of private individuals and other non-governmental organizations, such as TTSS, to working toward these goals as well. The Service notes that progress toward population objectives has been substantial, although not uniform throughout the range of the Rocky Mountain Population of Trumpeter swans. The Service additionally notes that this plan does establish goals and objectives for the Tristate area and supports the maintenance and enhancement of the breeding distribution of Trumpeter swans in both the Tristate and throughout the range of the currently recognized Rocky Mountain Population of Trumpeter swans. However, as described in the draft EA and several previous documents, efforts to achieve winter distributional objectives have not been as successful, despite considerable expenditures and intensive attempts to achieve these goals. The Service is contributing to the development of a new planning effort, in conjunction with its State, other Federal Agency, and private partners to determine how best to proceed to achieve these goals. Like TTSS, the Service is hopeful that the ongoing Implementation Plan process will lead to implementation of effective actions and some efforts are already underway.

2. TTSS states: "The winter vulnerability of the entire RMP has been described in numerous Service and Flyway reports, including the current Pacific Flyway RMP Management Plan. While the increase of Canadian trumpeters during recent mild winters is most welcome, their increasing concentration in high-risk habitat in eastern Idaho has compounded their vulnerability. Last year's surveys confirmed that virtually all (over 3,600) Canadian and Tristate trumpeters are stacking up in the Tristate wintering area. The seriousness of the situation was well described by Service Deputy Director Paul Schmidt during our TTSS Conference in 1999 when he stated "Despite the promising increase in RMP trumpeters, until we restore their migrations and help them return to more suitable wintering areas, their recovery will remain questionable." This coming winter, the vulnerability of the RMP will be unusually great, due to the worst regional drought since the1920s and the near total destruction of aquatic vegetation last winter at Harriman State Park."

The Service is concerned about and supportive of efforts to improve the wintering distribution of RMP Trumpeter swans. The Service provides a discussion of this issue in the EA (pg. 12). In essence, there is no disagreement about the desirability of improving the winter distribution of RMP Trumpeter swans. The reference to potential impacts of the current drought situation and the habitat conditions at Harriman State Park are not unlike comments made last year to the Service's proposed regulations and is discussed in the EA as well (pg. 12). With regard to the potential impact of the preferred alternative on the winter distribution problem, the Service re-iterates its assessment from the draft EA below.

Estimated Harvest impacts: Distribution: The restricted winter distribution of RMP Trumpeter swans continues, despite more than a decade of management actions intended to alter this situation. The fact that this problem has existed for more than a decade, that the population has continued to grow, and that no additional losses specifically attributable to severe winter weather conditions suggests to the Service that the threat to the population from the current winter distribution is perhaps overstated by some. This is not intended to suggest that the Service views the current winter distribution as desirable, nor that the Service is unaware that winter conditions have perhaps been more favorable than those historically experienced in this region. Regardless, the RMP has more than doubled in size since the 1989 winter die-off (Caithamer 2001) and should now be much better able to withstand winter losses without the threat of adverse impacts to the long-term welfare of the population as a whole. We would assume such losses would be distributed proportionally between the various components and thus winter losses of the magnitude that occurred in 1989 should be easily withstood by the population, and without jeopardy to the population as a whole or any identified component of the population.

At present, the Service is not aware of any effective methodology that will dramatically alter this winter distribution and notes that this problem is fairly common in waterfowl management. However, limited progress has been made toward improving the winter distribution (Bouffard 2000). The problem of wintering concentrations of both geese and swans either establishing or moving their wintering distribution further north is well documented. To date, it has proven beyond the capacity of managers to dramatically alter the winter distributions of waterfowl, despite several intensive and expensive efforts (Rusch et al. 1985; Shea and Drewien 1999). Therefore, the Service finds the limited changes in distribution that have been achieved to date encouraging, and suggests that perhaps such smaller, incremental improvements are really what is reasonable for management agencies to achieve. The Service has outlined it's plan for continuing efforts to achieve both status and distribution objectives (Appendix A) and is working with other partners to implement similar actions on lands not directly controlled by the Service. The Service feels such efforts can lead to further improvements and serve as mitigation for any limited negative impacts caused by maintaining an active Tundra swan hunting program.

The Service notes that exact knowledge of historical distributions and migration pathways is based on very limited evidence. The existing evidence is insufficient to determine if migration through the Great Salt Lake Basin was the only, or even the major migration pathway for Trumpeter swans associated with this area. There is little evidence that the Bear River area has ever been an important migration and/or wintering area for Trumpeter swans, and despite contentions to the contrary, the Service is aware of only a few confirmed records that document Trumpeter swans in this area throughout history. The Service would note that limited early banding of RMP Trumpeter swans near Grand Prairie, Alberta established the connection between that area and those Trumpeter swans wintering in the Tristate area, and also reported a limited number of recoveries from Nebraska, suggesting a more easterly migration path southward from the Tristate area (Mackay 1957). The Service also believes that migration southward through the Great Salt Lake Basin and perhaps westward following the Snake and then Columbia Rivers may well represent other historical migration routes. Further, the Service notes that the only current sustained southerly migration of RMP Trumpeter swans follows the Green River drainage through Wyoming and eastern Utah and is the direct result of active management efforts by the State of Wyoming (Bill Long, WY Game and Fish, pers. comm.). Therefore, the Service's conclusion is that a variety of potential southerly migration strategies through various areas are possible, and that the best possibilities for improving the winter distribution of RMP Trumpeter swans is further development and expansion of the approach used in Wyoming.

The issue that has been raised by some in discussions on the general impact of the Utah swan season, is that it is not the expected population effect of any harvest that is a matter of concern, but rather the potential impact of that limited harvest on redistribution efforts. Some have suggested that because Tundra swans stage at and migrate through Utah that this is the only reasonable avenue open to Trumpeter swans, currently concentrated north of this general area, however, as discussed above the Service does not subscribe to this view. Additionally, some have suggested that because those Trumpeter swans in Utah represent Trumpeter swans with a more desirable migration pattern, they should be protected from harvest at all cost.

It is the latter part of this contention that the Service feels is unjustified by the available data and the status of RMP Trumpeter swans (both in general and for all geographic components). There is no evidence, of which the Service is currently aware, to support the contention that the small numbers of Trumpeter swans being harvested in the Great Salt Lake Basin are serving as an impediment to a significant alteration in the migration patterns of RMP Trumpeter swans. The Service notes that RMP Trumpeter swans migrate through and are known to be present at Freezeout Lake in Montana, and despite the occasional harvest of some individual Trumpeter swans, there has been no discernable impact on either their migratory behavior or population status of Trumpeter swans. The Service opinion is that simply stopping the limited harvest in Utah will have little or no effect on the winter distribution of RMP Trumpeter swans, unless or until active management efforts lead to a general increase in the number of Trumpeter swans following this route. If such larger movements should happen, the Service is confident that the quota approach in existence will provide sufficient protection for dispersing swans to avoid undue adverse impacts at either the general population or any geographic component level (see also EA pgs. 42-45).

The Service recognizes that there is a difference of opinion with regard to this particular issue and would like to address a number of the contentions raised by those advocating this view. The Service gives little credence to the contention that loss of a few individual Trumpeter swans in Tundra swan seasons in Utah poses any threat to redistribution efforts. Regardless, in acknowledgment of those parties who believe differently, the Service imposed additional restrictions on the general swan season in Utah in 2000. These restrictions closed that portion of Utah to all swan hunting where 50% (7) of Trumpeter swans had been killed in the 5-year experimental swan season. In contrast BRMBR accounted for 21% (3) of the reported harvest during this period (Data supplied by the State of Utah). The additional restrictions also reduced the total number of swan hunting permits allocated to Utah from 2,750 to 2,000 and reduced the Trumpeter swan quota from 15 to 10 for the State. This reduction in quota was in recognition of the known difficulty in adjusting the number of swans checked for those wounded and lost, and for non-reporting by hunters. The questionnaire survey conducted after the close of the hunting season is used adjust for these two factors (see point 5 below). As stated previously, the Service feels that the information gained to date regarding the distribution of Trumpeter swans harvested in Utah suggests that Trumpeter swans were more likely to be encountered north of the BRMBR and associated with smaller wetland areas. The Service will continue to monitor the distribution of the swan harvest, in addition to the actual number of swans harvested in Utah.

3.   TTSS states: "Our foremost concern is to see effective actions taken to increase the winter distribution of the Canadian and Tristate trumpeters, and to reduce their high vulnerability. In 1995, The Trumpeter Swan Society's decision not to oppose experimental harvest of trumpeters was based solely on implementation of the entire proposed package of actions to benefit RMP winter range expansion that was presented to the public. TTSS agreed to remove hunter liability by legalizing quota harvest of trumpeters provided trumpeters were translocated into swan hunt areas south of the Tristate area. Although the hunt was implemented in 1995-2001, the other portions of the package to encourage the southward expansion of the RMP and improve security at Bear River Refuge were not. Despite implementation of the general hunt experiment, efforts to increase use of more southerly winter habitat have been stalled since 1997. To date, the generic swan hunting season has not benefitted southward expansion of the RMP, as was the original premise."

The Service is concerned about all aspects of the population health and welfare of the Rocky Mountain Population of Trumpeter swans and does not rank the winter distribution in advance of numeric status, for example. The Service and cooperators did attempt a number of efforts to alter the winter distribution of this population (see discussion to previous point), unfortunately these efforts met with only limited success as discussed throughout the draft EA. These actions did include translocations to Bear River Refuge, both during and after the swan hunting season. Although TTSS states that their support of the generic swan season was based solely on the desire to address the winter distribution issue, the Service and States also supported this approach for both this aspect and as a practical way to address the hunter liability issue and as a means to better monitor and control the harvest of Trumpeter swans in existing Tundra swan seasons in the Pacific Flyway. As stated in the draft EA, as Trumpeter swan populations continue to grow and expand throughout their range, this issue is expected to only increase over time and does require development of a practical and feasible approach for future harvest management of Tundra swan seasons. The Service does believe that this approach has been successful in addressing the liability and monitoring aspect, but would agree, and also states in the EA that harvest management alone will not solve the winter distribution situation of the Rocky Mountain Population of Trumpeter swans.

4.   TTSS states: Future RMP management strategies must recognize that to build substantial migrations out of eastern Idaho, it is critical to either protect the limited numbers of trumpeters that are currently migrating further south, or augment their numbers and provide adequate feeding areas and security so they can establish repeated use of new areas. Trumpeter Swan migration routes develop slowly. When the number of southward migrants is small, harvest of only a few pioneering birds each year can impede development of new traditions for southward winter expansion.

The Service supports the concept that development and enhancement of migratory traditions away from the current winter concentration area in southeastern Idaho are a key component of both existing and future management plans for RMP Trumpeter swans. The Service has also endorsed the concept of augmentation of the existing breeding component of the RMP in the Tristate area in such a fashion as to encourage the development of such migratory patterns and is currently supporting such efforts. The Service believes that the example program in the Green River Drainage implemented by the State of Wyoming is an approach that holds a promise for some success in this regard. The Service is committed to working with it's partner agencies and private interests to include this approach in the broader implementation plan currently in development. The harvest of small numbers of Trumpeter swans in existing swan hunting seasons is not viewed by the Service as detrimental to such efforts. The Service holds this view because of the expected low numeric impact (EA pgs. 42-45) and lack of evidence that small losses can be reasonably expected to alter migratory behavior (EA pg. 30).

5.   TTSS states: "We are still concerned about monitoring procedures to ensure that trumpeter harvest can be accurately documented and hunting can be closed promptly when quotas are met. Information received recently from the Service explained that: 1) There was no written Service Plan for monitoring and enforcement of the harvest quota for trumpeters. 2) Monitoring methods were left up to the states with no specific Service requirements or oversight, 3) One

checkstation was only run on parts of some days ("peak hunting hours") at Bear River Refuge, and 4) The 1932 Secretary's Regulation that previously required all hunters to check all birds harvested on the Refuge was changed "administratively" in 1995, coincident with the initial trumpeter quota harvest experiment, without disclosure in the 1995 swan hunt EA."

Further, with regard to this issue, TTSS states: "The Service has not yet explained, in this Draft EA or elsewhere, if any mandatory checkstations were conducted anywhere else in Utah and Nevada during the general swan hunt or what other methods were used to assure credible trumpeter harvest data in the quota hunt areas. It has become obvious, however, that mandatory check stations have only been rarely and, at best, intermittently implemented and well over 2,000 swans have been shot without determination of species since 1995 (Table 1). The lack of mandatory checkstations throughout the general hunt has been in marked contrast to Service policy in quota management for other species and ignores the clear guidance provided by the Service when the initial experiment was authorized. In the 1995 Federal Register summary, the Service pointedly instructed the swan hunt states that "If monitoring costs are prohibitive, consideration should be given to either increasing permit fees or having fewer hunt days in a week so as to reduce costs of operating check stations as is commonly done in several states that conduct controlled goose or crane hunts." Nevertheless, mandatory checkstations, with a prompt check requirement and enforcement were not implemented. As a consequence, the Service's Trumpeter Swan harvest data lack credibility and the Draft EA cannot meaningfully evaluate the impact of harvest on the pioneering trumpeters that are attempting to migrate southward."

The Service takes strong exception to the contention that the existing harvest data provided in the Draft EA lacks credibility or that the Service cannot meaningfully evaluate the impact of Trumpeter swan harvest. The Service manages all waterfowl cooperatively with States and other jurisdictions that share legislative mandates for the management of waterfowl. In establishing Federal Frameworks, the Service does also occasionally establish guidelines for monitoring of such seasons as it has done in this case . These guidelines have been clearly stated in both previous Environmental Assessments of this issue and in Federal Regulations (FR Vol. 65, No. 188, Wednesday, September 27, 2000:58152-58157). Individual refuge operations and procedures are the purview of the refuge and are not addressed in Federal Frameworks. All refuges develop and implement hunting regulations for their specific areas based on a separate Federal rule-making process, that is open to public comment and review. These regulations are consistent with or more restrictive than State regulations. The Service generally defers to States, but in some cases works closely with them, on implementation. This is done in recognition that States have the best local knowledge and logistical capability to accomplish these ends. In this case, the Service has evaluated the harvest data provided by the States and it's assessment is that reasonable diligence has been employed to this point, and that the data provided by the States is adequate to (a) monitor the take of Trumpeter swans during the season and (b) provide sufficient information to allow reasonable corrections for harvest losses that are not reported. The Service believes TTSS analysis is flawed for the following reasons. First, TTSS includes swans believed wounded and lost in their estimates of unreported swans. By definition, these swans are not retrieved and thus could not be checked by any known means. Wounding loss is an unfortunate reality of allowing hunting and the Service and State waterfowl managers have always taken this factor into account by expanding known losses by a factor for estimated wounding loss. Such expansions are estimates and the EA reports and uses this expansion in it's assessment of harvest. Second, TTSS refers to the difference between known checked birds and estimated (via a questionnaire survey) harvested birds as additional unchecked swans. Again, the Service believes that this estimate is biased high due to well documented deficiencies in questionnaire survey to estimate harvest (e.g. Rupp et al. 2000, Taylor et al. 2000, Cada 1983). In essence, unsuccessful hunters, those that fail to harvest a swan, are less likely to respond to a questionnaire survey, this leads to inflated estimates of actual harvest. The Service notes that the comment letters from the Pacific Flyway Council and the State of Utah provide actual data documenting this effect in this case and that both the Pacific and Central Flyways, as well as most individual States, recommended that further conditions on harvest monitoring not be imposed in those Pacific Flyway States as current information was adequate for management purposes.

The positions of the parties both for and against further Federal mandates for increased harvest monitoring have been carefully considered by the Service. Based primarily on the issue of whether or not current monitoring could act quickly to close the season should the quota in Utah be reached (something that the above review supports has not happened to date), coupled with the assessment below concluding that this is really only an issue in Utah, the Service has concluded that further requirements for swan harvest monitoring in Utah should be imposed, at least for the duration of the experimental period. Therefore, the Service will require Utah to enter into a Memorandum of Understanding (MOU) with the Service that agrees with the following further stipulations with regard to swan harvest monitoring in Utah: (1) Swans must be physically checked within seventy-two hours of harvest, (2) A commitment to enforce this regulation must be made by the State of Utah, (3) Utah hunters must hunt with their permit in their possession, and said permit must be validated with time and place swan is killed prior to removing the swan from the field, (4) Adequate State provisions must be in place to effect a prompt season closure should the quota be reached, and (5) at a minimum, a weekly summary of swan harvests will be made to the Service and the Service will be immediately notified should the harvest quota be reached. The Service will not authorize a swan hunting season in Utah without such an MOU.

The Service does state explicitly that it does not intend to require same day checks of swans in Utah in this MOU. The Service notes that no system can reasonably be considered entirely without error and the expectation that we can account for every swan harvested every day is not a feasible expectation. However, the Service does agree that a high level of real-time accountability is required of the harvest monitoring system in Utah. The Service assessment based on the above discussion is in general concurrence with the comments submitted by the State of Utah who stated that approximately 85-90% compliance with reporting requirements is currently being achieved. In addition there are procedures in place that allow a reasonable and likely conservative estimate of non-reported harvest and additionally provide annual estimates of wounding loss. Mandating same-day check-stations be operated at considerable cost can really be expected to gain at best only 10-15% in additional accountability. The Service reduction in Utah's quota from 15 to 10 more than compensates for any potential of this small level of non-reporting.

6.   TTSS states: "Our Board believes that the fundamental thrust of future RMP management efforts should be to expand fall/winter distribution of Trumpeter Swans (both Tristate and Canadian) directly south from eastern Idaho into

northern Utah, and possibly beyond. As the EA suggests, there are other possible routes, but these have been tried for a decade with little success. Agencies have spent great effort and expense attempting to rebuild a secure RMP winter distribution to less suitable habitats, and in less logical directions than directly south into Utah, in order to reduce possible conflicts with Tundra Swan hunting."

Further TTSS continues: "Successful use of new wintering areas has only occurred at the two release sites in Idaho and Wyoming that lie directly south of the Tristate area, where carrying capacity was unfortunately quite limited. Winter range expansion efforts should now progress further south and help trumpeters establish secure use of Bear River Refuge and adjacent areas without further delay. Bear River Refuge's Comprehensive Management Plan specifically says "In cooperation with the State of Utah and the Pacific Flyway Council, the Refuge will serve as a translocation site for migrating trumpeter swans. Activities aimed at moving Trumpeter Swans onto the Refuge will be done under an approved and coordinated plan." Bear River Refuge should be a cornerstone of any program to expand the winter distribution of the Trumpeter Swans and active involvement of this Refuge should proceed without further delay. We believe swan hunting has had a very significant negative impact on RMP range expansion efforts by preventing the effective use of this National Wildlife Refuge."

TTSS concludes their discussion of the aspect with: "We emphasize the importance of Bear River Refuge because of the Service's management authority, the Refuge's geographical proximity directly south of current trumpeter wintering areas, and its potential to provide secure and abundant sago pondweed habitat during fall migration and part or all of winter. Once the swan hunt ends in December south of the Refuge, migrant trumpeters could leave the Refuge in relative safety and disperse within Utah or beyond. Although the Draft EA is correct that records of historic trumpeter use at Bear River Refuge are sparse, trumpeter use has been documented from bones in Indian camps and live sightings, and early records were more frequent at Bear River than in any other portion of the Intermountain West outside the Tristate area. If Trumpeters Swans cannot be assisted to reestablish secure use of excellent historic habitat on a National Wildlife Refuge, a mere 100 miles south of current wintering sites, there is little chance that they will have better success in more distant habitats where the Service lacks the ability to provide abundant food and security."

The Service has stated above it's concurrence with the concept of expanding the winter distribution of RMP Trumpeter swans. The Service, however, views the focus on a particular place and/or direction as likely beyond the ability of managers to dictate. As the Service indicates in the draft EA, we know of no way to make these birds move, much less in a particular direction or to a specific place. We also contend that we have made considerable provisions, that should they move to Utah, they will have adequate access to sanctuary by closing the bulk of the State of Utah to all swan hunting and by providing extensive areas on Bear River Refuge that are closed to all hunting. The Service notes that the Central and Pacific Flyway Councils and several individual States have commented that the Service has gone too far to provide sanctuary for birds that show little inclination to migrate into this area. The Service would be very pleased to have significant numbers of Trumpeter swans migrate to Bear River Refuge. However, to date, the majority of Trumpeter swans remain in southeastern Idaho in winter. The Service also notes the previous discussion regarding where in Utah Trumpeter swans are known to have been harvested. The Service continues to believe closing BRMBR is not warranted based on the limited harvest data available. The Service again notes the only successful migratory group of Trumpeter swans outside the Tristate area is the result of the State of Wyoming's introduction efforts. The Service re-iterates its position that this approach is where the focus of future range expansion and population enhancement efforts should be.

7.   TTSS states: "Our Board is also concerned that the Draft EA fails to recognize the discreteness and biological importance of the Tristate nesting population. The Service has repeatedly emphasized that the RMP is a management-administrative entity, not a biological population. We concur. Use of this convenient administrative label, however, does not eliminate the need to also recognize biological populations, particularly when they face serious problems. Despite past casual use of names, the Tristate nesting trumpeters have been surveyed, modeled, and managed as a discrete biological population since their discovery over 80 years ago. Despite over 50 years of banding data, there is no evidence of successful interbreeding with the Canadian trumpeters that also winter in the Tristate area. The Tristate trumpeters are the only native nesting population in the lower 48 states that escaped extirpation and today they are the only viable nesting population in the western U.S. Outside of the Tristate region, there were only an additional 9 scattered nesting pairs in the entire western U.S. last year. Genetic studies during the 1990s by White and Marsolais (McMaster University, Ontario) found statistically significant genetic differences between the Tristate and Western Canadian trumpeters, which the EA does not mention. These genetic concerns were in part responsible for the State of Wyoming's insistence that the Tristate stock not be mixed with other stocks in their captive rearing facilities. While we hope that listing of the Tristate Population under the distinct population segment criteria of the ESA will not be necessary, we urge the Service to recognize the importance of this biological population and aggressively address the threats to its security. Referring to this biological population as a mere "flock" is inappropriate and obscures its discreteness and importance."

The Service addresses the issue of the petition to list a segment of the currently recognized Rocky Mountain Population of Trumpeter swans as a distinct population segment (EA pg. 3). The Service cannot comment on this issue further at this point. However, the Service would note that whether or not this petition is found to be warranted, it does not alter the fact that the winter distribution problem is common to all components of the Rocky Mountain Trumpeter Swan Population (excepting those nesting in Oregon and Nevada). Therefore, management needs and approaches to the winter situation will remain essentially unchanged.

8.   TTSS further states: However, we have found it very difficult to respond to this Draft EA because of substantial omissions of important data and numerous errors. These flaws confuse the discussion, lead to erroneous conclusions, and make meaningful comment difficult. To convey some sense of the magnitude of these problems, we cite some examples:

The Service appreciates the attention to detail given the draft EA in TTSS review. A number of more specific points are offered in addition to the more general comments addressed above. With regard to the more specific points, TTSS refers to "substantial omissions and numerous errors" in the draft. The Service response to this contention is as follows:

8. a.   TTSS contends that data from the 2000-2001 hunting season is missing.

The Service simply notes that all data available at the time the draft was prepared are presented in the draft. Since that time, the Service has received the additional data from Montana, Utah, and Nevada. This data documents a known harvest of four Trumpeter swans during the 2000-2001 hunting season, three in Montana and one in Utah (Tables 1a-1d, 2).

8. b.   TTSS contends that the Service did not disclose that it has not required mandatory check stations.

This point has been previously addressed, see discussion of point 5 of TTSS above.

8. c.   TTSS contends that there are errors in the population figures, the major reason for producing the updated draft. TTSS further refers to confusion regarding terminology for various population components within the Rocky Mountain Population of Trumpeter swans.

The Service strongly disagrees with the contention that it has inaccurately portrayed population data or trends (further discussion of this point under 8. d.). However, the Service does acknowledge difficulties regarding terminology throughout this entire process and believes that some contentions regarding population status are a function of this, rather than any disagreement about actual survey results. In an effort to clarify this aspect of the discussion, the Service adopted the terminology and definitions originally presented in the 1998 Pacific Flyway Management Plan (EA pg.10). In addition we have endeavored to clarify any points identified during the comment period in the final document.

8. d.   TTSS contends that RMP components and trends are inaccurately described.

The Service strongly disagrees with this contention. The 2000 survey (Caithamer 2001) numbers are not in dispute. The Survey clearly shows the continuing exponential growth of the Rocky Mountain Population of Trumpeter Swans and was contained by reference in the draft. As for the various components, the Service believes that TTSS comments are misleading and based on an arbitrary comparison of time periods that are not biologically meaningful in light of the question addressed by this EA, and the potential role of limited take of Trumpeter swans in Tundra swan seasons. The trend in numbers for this component is accurately presented in the EA (pg. 11), Trumpeter swan numbers declined during the winter of 1992/93 and have been recovering since, although they have not reached the levels present during the active winter feeding program. The Service does not believe that comparison to the 1968-85 period, when there was active winter feeding and prior to other active management efforts designed to alter the winter distribution, are meaningful in light of the fact that legal harvest of Trumpeter swans did not begin until 1995. The Service concludes that there is a significant possibility that winter habitat was substantially changed by discontinuation of the feeding program and other management activities. The count of this component of the RMP increased from 364 (1995) prior to the first experimental period in which the take of Trumpeter swans was allowed to 426 (2000) in the most recent 5-year survey.

This error, is really nothing more than a difference of opinion between the Service assessment and what TTSS believes is a meaningful time period for comparison.

There is an error in one sentence in the draft EA on page 11. The sentence should read: "Similarly, management activities undertaken in recent years apparently have not had the same impact on all components of this population." The Service has corrected this sentence and notes that the meaning should have been clear when the passage was taken in context of the additional discussion on page 11.

8. e.   TTSS contends that data and conclusions regarding past winter mortality are incorrect.

The Service again feels that this contention is taken out of context from the draft. The statement regarding winter mortality (EA pg. 5, Appendix B) made by the Service is: "The fact that this problem has existed for more than a decade, that the population has continued to grow, and that no additional losses specifically attributable to severe winter weather conditions...". The Service stands behind this statement, and to our knowledge there were no appreciable numbers of dead swans found at HSP after the winter of 1989, although we acknowledge that some birds are found dead almost every year. The Service also notes and discusses the apparent loss of substantial numbers of swans associated with the core Tristate area during the winter of 1992/93. The cause of this apparent mortality is unknown and cannot be attributed to severe winter weather conditions to our knowledge. The Service does not believe that conjecture as to the specific cause(s) of this decline is warranted.

8. f.   TTSS contends that conclusions regarding attainment of Flyway Management Plan objectives are incorrect.

There is some merit to this contention by TTSS, however, the Service would again note the following. The Service took as the basis for this comparison the figures provided in a Table on page 13 of the Pacific Flyway Management Plan entitled "1997 Population levels and short-term (2002) objectives". This Table does not include the modifier minimum. However, the Service acknowledges 2 points, the first that there is verbiage on page 12 related to numbers of nesting pairs stating: "Objective 2 is to rebuild U.S. breeding flocks by year 2002 to at least 131 nesting pairs", and additionally, there is a footnote on the Table that does refer to limiting the population plan objectives labeled as adults and subadults to white birds. The Service provided figures that included young of the year in the draft (including them as subadults) and TTSS is correct that by this criteria of the plan as defined in the Table footnote, the number should be 324 and the appropriate percentage 68% of objective (324/480). The Service appreciates the attention to detail paid by TTSS, but hopes that this focus does not detract from the main point intended by the Service in this section, that there is a finite limit to what population growth can be reasonably expected in this area and that numbers of Trumpeter swans have increased in both the RMP and the Tristate breeding component of this population during the period of the experimental hunt allowing the legal take of Trumpeter swans. TTSS acknowledged this continued growth in it's comment, although they caution this acknowledgment by qualifying statements regarding recent years as more favorable than average for recruitment. The Service would also emphasize the point that population growth is most likely influenced by a variety of factors unrelated to hunting programs. Therefore, the Service fully expects fluctuations in population growth over time caused by such things as local habitat and weather conditions. The Service's point here is that during the period in which a limited take was allowed, growth did occur, supporting the Service's position that limited harvest is not inconsistent with population growth.

9. TTSS contends that although the Draft EA states that "constraints imposed upon swan hunting seasons described in the Supplemental Environmental Assessment on this issue (Trost et al. 2000) would be continued", later statements contradict this. The Draft EA actually increases the period a hunter has to check a swan (Utah had been allowing up to 72 hours, the Draft EA allows up to 5 calendar days), and lengthens the season in Nevada by about a week. Such modifications should have been made clear to the public.

The Service notes that: (1) the reporting time of 72 hours was one established by Utah, not the Federal regulation last year and (2) the regulations proposed for Nevada are intended to be the same as last year, as presented in the Table comparing alternatives. The closing date restriction in the text has been corrected to the first Sunday following January 1st in Nevada. The Service will formalize a specific MOU with the State of Utah establishing the necessary monitoring requirements and procedures for season closure should the Trumpeter swan quota be reached as described above.

10. In conclusion, TTSS makes two recommendations: (1) to withdraw from the current EA process and to then implement a variation on Alternative 2, return to a Tundra swan only hunt, however, with numerous additional conditions that were not part of the hunt as it was conducted historically, or (2) add a new alternative to the EA process for consideration (and selection as the preferred alternative), the new alternative being essentially the same as is recommended in the first alternative by TTSS.

The Service has no basis on which to withdraw from the current EA process and continue to offer hunting seasons on Tundra and/or Trumpeter swans in the Pacific Flyway and believes that this process has served well to provide sufficient alternatives for future management of these seasons. The Service does not see the offered alternative as providing any appreciable new courses of action to the existing alternatives. Additionally, inclusion of a new alternative, essentially alternative 2 with numerous new conditions, seems without merit in light of the recognized identification problem.

The first issue applicable to the current swan season in the three affected States is whether a return to Tundra swan only hunting seasons regardless of their structure, would be of any benefit to either population or distribution concerns for Trumpeter swans. The Service feels that we must acknowledge the reality that discrimination between the two species by hunters in the field will never be absolute. The Service has worked with the States to develop hunter education materials to help reduce the misidentification problem, and will continue with these efforts. The Service specifically notes the offer by the State of Utah in their comments to implement a mandatory swan identification program for all first time swan hunters and will work with Utah to see such a program is implemented. However, the Service position is that there will always be some degree of misidentification, and that sound management must acknowledge this issue and deal with it. Therefore, the Service continues to believe that promulgation of regulations that it knows will be ineffective is not a reasonable course of action. Additionally, the Service does not feel that hunters should be held liable for what almost all biologists agree is an unreasonable expectation that they be able to discriminate between these two species in hunting situations. The Service would further note the following points as how it assessed these recommendations by TTSS on a State by State basis (see also EA pgs. 4-5).

A.   TTSS or others offer no reason why the preferred alternative should not be adopted in Montana. There is no question that some Trumpeter swans are taken in this season, but the Service position that these individuals are most likely associated with the expanding segment that breeds in Canada and the hunt area has no influence on the current winter distribution problem that TTSS identifies as it's major concern. Restriction of this season to Tundra swan hunting only based on possible population impacts to Trumpeter swans or impacts on Trumpeter swan winter distribution do not seem warranted and have not been suggested by TTSS or others. Consequently the Service sees nothing in the comments that suggest alteration of this season is needed at this time.

B.   TTSS does suggest that potential harvest of Trumpeter swans in Nevada is a problem, and the Service interpretation of this position is that this is because any swans harvested in Nevada would (or could) be dispersing swans from the problem winter concentration area and should be protected at all costs to foster this behavior. However, the Service notes that only one Trumpeter swan is known to have been harvested in Nevada in 7 years. Additionally, compliance rates have been extremely high to harvest surveys in Nevada and even expanded for estimated wounding loss and non-compliance to harvest surveys the Service must conclude that the number of Trumpeter swans at risk in this season has been so low that any potential impact seems very remote. This coupled with the fact that the Service and State of Nevada have introduced Trumpeter swans to the State and thus these introduced swans are as, if not more, likely the source of the swan(s) currently being harvested there leads the Service to conclude that there is simply no evidence that suggests that the preferred alternative is not the appropriate course of action in Nevada at this time. In essence the question the Service would ask is: Should the State of Nevada pay for it's efforts to help Trumpeter swan restoration by further restricting or closing it's swan hunting season ?

C.   Finally, the Service considered the situation in Utah. The Service believes that this State's hunting season, conducted immediately south of the problem winter concentration area, is really the core issue in all of comments from groups and organizations opposed to the Service's preferred alternative, that do not base such opposition on a general objection to swan hunting. The Service considered this question from two aspects: (1) potential population impacts (see following), and (2) potential impacts on redistribution efforts (see point 2 above).

Estimated Harvest impacts: Numeric: The Service believes that the continued increase in the RMP of Trumpeter swans is clear evidence that the limited harvest currently occurring is not a threat to continued growth in this population. During the five-year period of the first experimental hunt (1995-1999), a total of 32 Trumpeter swans were known to have been harvested by hunters in Montana, Utah, and Nevada (Table 2, revised to remove Trumpeters estimated from the Central Flyway portion of Montana as per comments received from Flyway Councils and States). Four additional Trumpeters are known to have been shot in the Pacific Flyway in the 2000-2001 season (Table 2) and one was known to have been harvested in Montana in the 1994-1995 season, prior to the implementation of the original experiment. Thus a total of 37 Trumpeter swans are known to have been harvested during the period 1994-95 through

2000-2001 (7 years). Expanding this number for both noncompliance (non-reporting) and wounding loss, suggests that as many as 49 Trumpeter swans may have been harvested in the Pacific Flyway (7 per year). Of these, 53% or 26 were estimated to have been taken in Montana, with the remaining 23 estimated taken in Utah (22) and Nevada (1).

The Service notes that the segment of the population that has been proposed for listing also increased in number during the period of legal Trumpeter swan harvest, suggesting no negative impacts of either of the harvest management regimes that have been employed during the past 6 years. An issue concerning the U.S. flocks that is related to those who express concerns for this component of the population is the question of what is a reasonable objective for numbers in this region. The Pacific Flyway Management Plan (Pacific Flyway Council 1998) established an objective of 480 total Trumpeter swans by 2002 for Trumpeter swans nesting in Montana, Wyoming, and Idaho. The most recent survey results (Reed 2000) for this area suggests that numbers have made progress toward this level since the winter of 1992-93 (324/480 = 68%). This objective level was established based on historic population levels and consideration of the habitat limitations of this region in conjunction with the possible lowered carrying capacity of this environment because of the cessation of winter feeding programs (e.g. see Banko 1960 for an early discussion regarding the believed carrying capacity of this general area).

The Service generally concurs with the objectives established by the Pacific Flyway Council while noting that more long-term numeric expansion may be possible by natural or management efforts to either improve habitat and/or introduce Trumpeter swans into presently unoccupied suitable habitats within these three States. It is the Service's intent to work toward further population expansion and has requested State and other Agencies to help develop a more detailed implementation plan of specific actions that will contribute toward this end (2000, FR Vol. 65, No. 188, Wednesday, September 27, 2000:58152-58175) . The Service has completed a draft plan that details some of the specific actions that the Service is considering to accomplish this end (Appendix A) and will continue to work with other interested agencies and organizations directly and through the Pacific Flyway Council to develop a comprehensive plan to accomplish this goal. However, the Service wishes to make clear that it does not expect to have unlimited growth of Trumpeter swans in this or any other habitat in the future and believes any such contention to be without biological foundation.
The Service believes that the vast majority, if not all, of the Trumpeter swan harvest in the Montana season is derived from the rapidly expanding northern breeding flocks of the RMP because the area open to hunting in Montana is generally north of the Core Tristate area and few if any Trumpeter swans are expected to migrate northward during the fall. Continued numeric and geographic growth of these flocks supports the Service position that such harvest levels pose no threat to this component of the population and that is why Montana is exempt from an actual assigned quota. This is not intended to imply that, should harvest monitoring programs and population information suggest that adjustment to this season are needed to maintain the long-term trend, the Service would not consider alterations to these seasons. However, the overwhelming evidence at this time supports the Service conclusion that this is not the case.

With regard to seasons in Nevada, few, if any, comments (with the exception of those opposed to all swan hunting addressed above) have suggested that harvest in Nevada is of any concern. Only a single Trumpeter swan is known to have been harvested in the past 7 years and there is no evidence that the season as it exists places any number of Trumpeter swans at risk. Therefore, the existing season in Nevada is not presently considered an issue that needs to be addressed. This is not intended to imply that, should harvest monitoring programs and population information suggest that adjustment to this season are needed to maintain the long-term trend, the Service would not consider alterations to these seasons. However, the overwhelming evidence supports the conclusion that this is not needed to address concerns regarding population status or distribution of Trumpeter swans at this time.

Therefore, it is, as indicated above, the harvest in Utah that the Service believes is the main issue to those whose concerns are not based on anything other than a general objection to the hunting of swans (or specifically Trumpeter swans) as addressed above. Harvest in Utah could include representatives from both Canadian and Tristate breeding flocks and also represents Trumpeter swans moving south out of the Tristate region, thus beginning a more desirable migration tradition. The Service has considered both aspects of this situation as follows.

First, the Service remains confident that the numeric losses that can be reasonably expected from the current hunting regime will have no impact from an overall population perspective. Estimated total RMP Trumpeter swan harvest has averaged 7 birds per year over the past 7 years in these three States and the total population has continued to grow steadily, supporting this conclusion. Additionally, any harvest losses in Utah can most reasonably be expected to be equal to the relative proportion that each breeding flock contributes to the population as a whole. The Service believes this to be a conservative approach because some have suggested that Tristate birds are less likely to migrate than Trumpeter swans from northerly breeding areas that migrate to the Tristate area each year. If this were true, the actual proportion of Tristate birds in the Utah and Nevada harvest would be even less. Therefore, losses in Utah are expected to be approximately 90% Canadian flocks and approximately 10% derived from the Tristate breeding flocks. This in turn equates to a maximum take from the Core Tristate area of approximately 2 individuals per year under a worst case scenario. This estimate is based on what the Service feels is the most reasonable projection and assumes that the quota is actually reached. The Service notes that the quota has never been reached in either Utah or Nevada during the last 7 years. Based on estimated actual harvest (known harvest inflated for both non-compliance and wounding loss) the estimated loss of Tristate Trumpeter swans for the period 1994-2001 (7 seasons) would thus be approximately two individuals (23 X 10% = 2.3) during this period. Based on this assessment, and as previously stated (FR Vol. 65, No. 188, Wednesday, September 27, 2000:58152-58175), the Service does not consider the expected level of harvest to be a significant threat to RMP Trumpeter swans in general, or to any individual component of this population proposed by any of the comment letters received or in the listing petition currently under consideration by the Service.

The Service conclusion is that current harvest levels are not a threat to the Rocky Mountain Population of Trumpeter swans continued growth and expansion, nor do these harvest levels pose a threat to any group or segment within the Rocky Mountain Population that has been suggested for separate consideration in the comments received. The Service does acknowledge there is a difference of opinion associated with regard to potential impacts on winter range expansion. The Service assessment is that the current season structure in Utah provides sufficient sanctuary areas for Trumpeter swans, that losses of a few individual Trumpeter swans in these seasons will not likely result in any appreciable impact on Trumpeter swan distributions, and that the current quota system will protect Trumpeter swans if there is any appreciable movement of these swans during the hunting season into Utah. Additionally, the Service is actively supporting efforts to rear and release additional Trumpeter swans in suitable habitat throughout the Pacific Flyway. These efforts are intended to help increase numbers of Trumpeter swans nesting in the conterminous United States and such introductions are also intended to build on the limited success of the Wyoming program to establish new breeding components with migratory traditions away from the core Tristate area.

In conclusion, the Service appreciates the attention and effort given by TTSS to provide meaningful comments to the draft EA. The Service does takes some exception to specific points raised by TTSS in their letter. However, the Service believes there is substantial agreement between the Service and TTSS with regard to management goals and objectives for this population of swans. The Service looks forward to working with TTSS and it's other partner agencies and organizations to further develop and implement the implementation plan to achieve the goals and objectives of the 1998 Pacific Flyway Management Plan for the Rocky Mountain Population of Trumpeter swans.

Several other agencies, organizations, and individuals sent comments consistent with those of TTSS. These include, Schubert and Associates (on behalf of FFA, HSUS, and BLF), the Friends of Animals (FOA), the State of Idaho (Department of Parks and Recreation), the Greater Yellowstone Coalition, Public Employees for Environmental Responsibility, the Utah Environmental Congress, the Friends of the West, the Idaho Conservation League, the Salish and Kootenai Tribes, and 143 individuals. There are a few points raised in these comments not raised by TTSS and the Service response to these points follows:

1.   The FFA and others suggest that this issue requires an Environmental Impact Statement be prepared regarding this issue.

The Service addresses this issue in it's Finding of No Significant Impact and decision document regarding this Environmental Assessment.

2.   The Confederated Salish and Kootenai Tribes include in their comments a concern for the potential of the preferred alternative to impact their restoration efforts on Tribal lands.

This issue is an example of the management scale question faced by all Service harvest management decisions and is closely related to the concerns expressed by Yellowstone National Park (see discussion following). The Service assessment of potential numeric impacts of the limited take of Trumpeter swans in the existing Tundra swan hunting seasons was conducted at both the total population level (as presently recognized) and considering the potential recognition of a distinct population segment affiliated with the Tristate area. At neither of these levels does the Service analysis support the contention that any negative impacts can reasonably be expected by implementation of the preferred alternative. The Service greatly appreciates and supports the efforts of the Confederated Salish and Kootenai Tribes to establish a breeding component of Trumpeter swans on their lands. In the view of the Service, the probability that one of these individual swans will migrate into a hunt area and be shot is very low and does not justify the elimination of several States swan hunting seasons. However, the Service does encourage the Tribe to leg-band all released swans and if any evidence from recoveries suggests more than a rare occurrence of harvest, the Service will work with the Tribe to ensure remedial action is taken.

3.   A letter was received from the Public Employees for Environmental Responsibility (PEER) that offered a number of comments, many pertaining to the issue regarding the listing petition that has been received by the Service and is addressed in the response to TTSS comments. In addition, PEER called into question the adequacy of the Service actions with regard to the NEPA process itself in addressing this issue. In addition they question whether or not science as opposed to political opinion has served as the basis for the Service actions.

The Service takes strong exception to the contention that it's intent with regard to this issue is not to meet both the intent and spirit of all applicable laws and regulations regarding the decision making process. The Service points out that this is the third Environmental Assessment the Service has prepared on this issue since 1995. All of these actions have included opportunities for public comment, public hearings were held in both Idaho and Utah on this issue, and extensive consultation with both public and private interests has occurred throughout the past several decades. In addition, each year since 1995 the Service has proposed specific regulations based on these Environmental Assessments and has accepted public comments through the Federal Register process established for this purpose. The Service views the contention that the Service's goal has been to gather a minimum of public input as unwarranted and unjustified as clearly demonstrated by the administrative record. The Service also strongly refutes the assertion that the Service has not used the best science in it's evaluation of potential impacts of the proposed hunting seasons on both the Rocky Mountain Population of Trumpeter swans and the Western Population of Tundra swans. The Service notes that no sources of additional data or information are suggested by PEER that would shed additional, objective light on this issue that are not included either directly or by reference in the draft EA. PEER offers no examples of how the existing data have been analyzed in any fashion that is not consistent with established wildlife management practices or what it believes constitutes a political versus a biological assessment. The Service notes that it has addressed the question of whether or not Trumpeter swans in the Tristate area should be considered a distinct population segment in it's response to TTSS above. However, the Service notes that it has assessed the numerical and distributional aspects of the proposed preferred alternative on both the Rocky Mountain Population as currently recognized and with regard to the Tristate breeding segment. In this and previous documents the Service has presented it's assessment of the genesis of the current distribution problem. The Service readily acknowledges that biologists opinions differ on the role of the proposed swan hunting seasons on the status and distribution of RMP Trumpeter swans, that is why the Service is again evaluating this issue again in this Environmental Assessment. The comments received to this effort clearly document these differences of opinion, despite general agreement on the actual biological data available for assessment. The Service has conducted a thorough assessment of all the available data and has based it's recommended preferred alternative on this evaluation.

4.   In addition, PEER poses a specific question: How does the Service intend to comply with NEPA and NWRS planning policies on the Implementation Plan ?

A number of issues are involved in this question. First, the Implementation Plan was requested by the Service of the Pacific Flyway Council and as such, it is not a Service plan. This request was made because of comments received to the previous Environmental Assessment that suggested actual means and activities intended to meet the goals and the objectives of the 1998 Pacific Flyway Management Plan were vague or undocumented. The Service supported this recommendation and in recognition of the fact that the Implementation Plan is intended to implement the existing Flyway Management Plan, the Service requested the Pacific Flyway Council undertake this further development of their management plan. The Service does have a role to play in this process but recognizes that States, other Federal agencies, private interests, and in this case Canada all have a stake and role to play in the management of this population as well. The Flyway Councils, an organization of States and Provinces, were created expressly to coordinate migratory bird management activities between all the various entities with legislative mandates for migratory bird management and the Federal governments which have the ultimate authority in all countries that are signatories to the Migratory Bird Treaty. This is not intended to imply or suggest that activities that are proposed for National Wildlife Refuges based on the results of this planning process will not be throughly addressed by all existing NEPA and planning policies which are applicable. The Service policy in this regard is to conduct such assessment when actions are actually funded for implementation and at the specific sites at which implementation is being considered.   Since such actions are currently being assessed in relation to other actions by the Implementation Planning effort, at this point the Service does not know which of the actions proposed by the various refuges that have submitted their proposed activities will be recommended for implementation. The Service believes that a planning process that examines all possible actions, including those on all public (whether administered by the Service or other governmental agencies) and private lands, will better serve to direct limited resources to those activities that are deemed by all the concerned interests to best meet the goals and objectives of the referenced Flyway Management Plan. The Service recognizes that this assessment may result in recommendations that do not include NWR actions at all, or only a subset of the actions currently proposed.   Of course, individual Refuges will be free to pursue such actions as they individually deem appropriate and such actions will obviously adhere to all applicable rules, policies and regulations.

5.   Twenty-six individuals from Canada commented in opposition to the Services preferred alternative and in general opposition to swan hunting.

Although these comments were not generally different than those offered by some United States citizens opposed to swan hunting in general, they did allude to several specific issue regarding the status and management of Trumpeter swans in Canada. The Service notes that Province of Alberta has replied to such inquiries with a letter of general support for implementation of the preferred alternative and that the Province of Alberta currently serves as the chair of the Central Flyway Council who also wrote in support of maintaining (actually increasing) existing hunting opportunities.

Comments generally neutral with regard to the preferred alternative but raising other issues regarding Tundra/Trumpeter swan management in the Pacific Flyway.

1.   Yellowstone National Park wrote expressing concerns about the status of Trumpeter swans associated with the Park.

The Service appreciates the comments of Yellowstone National Park and generally agrees with the points they offer. The Service agrees that maintenance and enhancement of the number of Trumpeter swans associated with Yellowstone National Park must be a key component of the implementation plan being developed. The Service concurs with the goals and objectives for nesting Trumpeter swans in this region established in the 1998 Flyway Plan. The Service is committed to work closely with the Park to implement any and all such actions that will help achieve this end. The Service understands that swans associated with the Park may have never migrated far from the core Tristate area. While noting that such behavior will serve to help protect these individuals from any remote possibility of harvest in areas outside the core Tristate area, the Service also acknowledges the need to maintain the diversity of migratory behaviors in Trumpeter swans throughout their range. We will work with the Park to build this component of the overall RMP. Finally, the Service is committed to comprehensive monitoring of any and all ongoing management activities and will strive to use the best science to address the challenges of managing this diverse population of swans.

2.   The Bureau of Reclamation (BOR) recommended a strong commitment to harvest monitoring and raised a question regarding the source of Trumpeter swans to be used in the introduction of Trumpeter swans into new areas proposed by the Service.

The Service appreciates the comments of the BOR regarding harvest monitoring and has detailed its intent to work with the State of Utah to develop a more clear and comprehensive plan for harvest monitoring through a new MOU above. In addition, the Service acknowledges the point made by BOR regarding the potential to further complicate the uncertain situation regarding the possible genetic integrity of subsets of swans associated with specific areas throughout the range of the RMP. The Service appreciates this concern and will not introduce any swans into the core Tristate area or the Tristate region that are not known to be derived from swans known to have originated from within the same area. If such introductions are to be done by the Service, we will conduct any separate NEPA assessments required.

3.   The Wildlife Management Institute (WMI) commented that the EA was similar to the previous 1995 and 2000 EA's on the same subject and felt that too much emphasis was placed on hunting regulations and too little on the broader management questions.

The Service agrees that all three of the environmental assessments have been similar, because they deal with the same issue and because not much new information, nor many new opinions have been offered with regard to this long-standing situation. The EA does focus primarily on the impacts of the proposed hunting seasons, because that is the purpose of the EA, to help determine what the appropriate hunting regulations for swans should be in those portions of Montana, Utah, and Nevada open to swan hunting. It is not the Service intent to conduct an exhaustive NEPA evaluation of different management strategies for Tundra and Trumpeter swans in the Pacific Flyway, as indicated in our response to PEER, the Service policy is to conduct NEPA assessment on actions not plans. The Service has included swan management issues only to the extent necessary to place the hunting season issue into context of the management of these two populations.

4.   The WMI was among several to comment on the drought conditions presently existing in the west should be considered in the Service decision on appropriate action.

The Service has considered the potential impact of the current drought conditions (EA pg. 12). The Service is hopeful that the poor conditions at HSP in particular lead to a broader dispersal of Trumpeter swans from this general area this winter. If this does occur, and Trumpeter swans disperse into areas open to hunting during the hunting season, the Service is confident that the existing quota system and large expanses of area closed to all swan hunting in northern Utah will provide sufficient protection for these individuals.

Comments generally in support of the preferred alternative or requesting reduction in various constraints imposed on existing swan hunting seasons.

The States of Wyoming, Oregon, Utah, Nevada, Idaho (Department of Fish and Game), the Pacific and Central Flyway Councils, the Conservation Force (on behalf of the Dallas Safari Club, Dallas Ecological Foundation, Houston Safari Club, African Safari Club of Florida, the Louisiana Chapter of the Safari Club International, the National Taxidermist Association, and the Central Louisiana Chapter of Safari Club International), the Nevada Waterfowl Association and 6 individuals wrote in support of continuation and/or expansion of existing swan hunting opportunities.

The Service responds to specific points raised in these comments as follows:

1.   The Service should make the Utah season operational and re-open the areas closed to swan hunting in the 2000 EA.

The Service has presented its assessment of both the numeric and distributional potential impacts of the existing swan seasons for each of the three States affected by the proposed alternative (points A, B, and C pg. 42 this EA). The Service notes that the time frame of this EA is for the next 2 hunting seasons. The Service continues to believe that an experimental status is appropriate in Utah to: (1) assess the impact of closing the areas north of BRMBR to all swan hunting, (2) Determine if the newly required monitoring actions in Utah are successfully implemented, and (3) allow time for completion of the requested implementation planning process. The Service assessment is that it would be premature to adopt an operational season in Utah at this time.

2.   Several States and both the Central and Pacific Flyway Councils recommended that no further conditions be imposed on harvest monitoring requirements in any of the current swan seasons.

The Service has carefully considered all aspects of the current harvest monitoring as described in the response to TTSS and others who recommended further conditions be imposed (point 5, pg. 33 this EA). The Service conclusion is to require development of a specific MOU with the State of Utah for harvest monitoring during the Utah season (pg. 35 this EA). The Service believes that it is necessary to insure that the existing quota system will serve to act promptly to close the season if the quota is reached in Utah. Based on the Service assessment of existing seasons in Montana and Nevada, the Service concludes that existing procedures are adequate to monitor the swan harvest in these States.

3.   The Pacific Flyway and several States took issue with the statement that the Service would work to "enhance trumpeter swan status and distribution within the Pacific Flyway ...". The State of Utah, in similar comments, also alluded to the establishment of a "Safe Harbor" agreement with cooperating States to help insure States that efforts to restore Trumpeter swans would not lead to further

restrictions in hunting opportunities. Finally, the State of Wyoming stated that $1.9 million of primarily sport license revenues had been expended by their State to help Trumpeter swan restoration during the past several decades. Wyoming suggested that further expenditures may be eliminated or severely restricted if the end result of such efforts was to be further restrictions on swan hunting opportunities in Pacific Flyway States.

The Service understands the concerns of the States and gratefully acknowledges the contribution of many of the States that have commented to Trumpeter swan restoration and enhancement over the past several decades. The Service notes that "Safe Harbor" agreements are specific, at this time, to issues related to species listed as Threatened or Endangered under ESA. The Service concurs with the concept of development of such a policy to that would allow the Service, States and private interests to enter into such agreements for species with special management concerns that are not listed under ESA. However, at this time, the Service has no such policy and thus lacks the ability to enter into such an agreement as suggested by the State of Utah. As a result of this request, the Service will seriously investigate the development and implementation of such a policy/procedure. Finally, the Service notes that the Implementation Plan process is intended to identify places and actions that will best suit the needs and interests of all the constituencies with an interest in Trumpeter swan management. The Service understands that the States are uncomfortable with reintroductions or introductions into areas where additional conflicts with swan hunting seasons may arise. The Service believes that there are sufficient alternatives available to avoid such direct conflicts and will strive for concurrence with all parties in deciding what actions to implement.

Summary

In conclusion, the Service has independently assessed the information available and has concluded that the preferred alternative will not significantly impact Trumpeter or Tundra swans in the Pacific Flyway. The relatively small number of Trumpeter swans that the Service expects to be harvested by this action will not pose a significant risk to either the Rocky Mountain Population as a whole, or any segment of this population that has been identified by others to this point. The Service recognizes that there are many challenges still present in developing and implementing a broad scale management program for Trumpeter swans in the Pacific Flyway. The Service will continue to work with interests to ensure the continued growth of this population. The Service is committed to meeting the goals and objectives of the 1998 Pacific Flyway Management Plan for this population of Trumpeter swans, including all of the Regional and State specific objectives. The Service is strongly committed to maintaining and enhancing Trumpeter swan numbers throughout the Tristate region, including those associated with Yellowstone National Park, and should new evidence become available that suggests that efforts to maintain and enhance these Trumpeter swans are being jeopardized by existing hunting seasons the Service will modify or suspend these seasons to ensure no adverse impacts are manifested. The Service does not find the existing evidence supports the contention of some parties that these existing seasons are currently having a significant impact either numerically or in influencing winter distributions of Trumpeter swans. In addition, the Service feels the active program proposed for direct augmentation of the Core Tristate Area nesting Trumpeter swans will offset any potential negative impacts caused by adopting the preferred alternative.

VI.   CONSULTATION AND COORDINATION

ENVIRONMENTAL ASSESSMENT - June 15, 2001

This Environmental Assessment is an expanded and revised version of two previous Environmental Assessments (Bartonek et al. 1995, Trost et al. 2000). Extensive consultations were conducted in the development and implementation of these original Environmental Assessments. Previous consultations are summarized in those documents. Service representatives have conducted discussions in conjunction with annually scheduled Flyway meetings and at the Trumpeter Swan Society Conference, September 15-18, 1999, in Idaho Falls, Idaho, where this issue was discussed at length. Additional input has been received from numerous groups and organizations. Two public meetings were held in Idaho Falls, Idaho and Salt Lake City, Utah specifically to accept public comments on the Supplemental Environmental Assessment prepared for the 2000-2001 hunting season. The Service met with members of the Bureau of Reclamation, the National Park Service, and representatives of the Biological Resources Division of USGS to discuss matters pertaining to this assessment in May of 2001. The Service has continued to receive comment on the issue of management of RMP Trumpeter swans from various public and private sources and has considered those comments in preparing this assessment.

A.   ENDANGERED SPECIES

Consultation under Section 7 of the Endangered Species Act of 1973, as amended (16 U.S.C. 1531 et seq.) has not been sought in development of this proposal but will be done during the regulatory process of developing frameworks for the 2001-2002 Migratory Game Bird Hunting Regulations. The proposed action is not likely to jeopardize the continued existence of listed species or result in the destruction or adverse modification of their critical habitats. Hunting regulations are designed, among other things, to remove or alleviate chances of conflict between seasons for migratory game birds and the protection and conservation of endangered and threatened species and their habitats. The Service's biological opinions resulting from its consultation under Section 7 are considered public documents and are available for inspection in the Division of Endangered Species and the Division of Migratory Bird Management.

B.   NEPA

NEPA considerations associated with the annual regulation setting process are covered by the programmatic document, ``Final Supplemental Environmental Impact Statement: Issuance of Annual Regulations Permitting the Sport Hunting of Migratory Birds (FEIS 88-14),'' filed with EPA on June 9, 1988. Notice of Availability was published in the Federal Register on June 16, 1988 (53 FR 22582). The Service's Record of Decision was published on August 18, 1988 (53 FR 31341). However, this programmatic document does not prescribe year-specific regulations; those are developed annually. The annual regulations and options that will be considered in the Environmental Assessment, which will assess the environmental impacts associated with development of the ``Waterfowl Hunting Regulations for 2001,'' will be available in September of 2001.

C.   PRINCIPAL PREPARERS

1.   Robert E. Trost, Pacific Flyway Representative, Division of Migratory Bird Management, U.S. Fish and Wildlife Service, 911 NE 11th Ave., Portland, Oregon 97232. Telephone: (503) 231-6162.

2.   Jon Andrew, Chief, Division of Migratory Bird Management, U.S. Fish and Wildlife Service, Washington, D.C. 20240. Telephone: (703) 358-1714.

3.   Robert J. Blohm, Division of Migratory Bird Management, U.S. Fish and Wildlife Service, Washington, D.C. 20240. Telephone: (703) 358-1714.

VII.   REFERENCES

American Ornithologists' Union. 1983. Check-list of North American Birds. 7th Edition American Ornithologist's Union, Washington, D.C.

Bartonek, J. C., R. Kokel, R. J. Blohm, and P. R. Schmidt. 1995. Environmental Assessment: Proposal to establish general swan hunting seasons in parts of the Pacific Flyway for the 1995-99 seasons. USFWS. 35pp. (Plus appendices)

Cada, J.D. 1983. Evaluations of the telephone and mail survey methods of obtaining harvest data from licensed sportsmen in Montana. Pages 117-128 in S.L Beasom and S.E. Roberson, eds. Game harvest management. Caesar Kleberg Res. Inst., Kingsville, Texas.

Caithamer, D. F. 2001. Trumpeter swan population status, 2000. U.S. Fish and Wildlife Service, Division of Migratory Bird Management. 14pp.

Banko, W. E. 1960. The Trumpeter Swan, it's history, habits and population in the United States. North American Fauna Number 63. U. S. Fish and Wildlife Service. U.S. Government Printing Office, Washington D.C.

Bouffard, S. H. 2000. Recent changes in winter distribution of RMP Trumpeter Swans. Pages 53-59 in Shea, R. E., M.H. Linck, and H. K. Nelson, eds. Proceedings and papers of the seventeenth Trumpeter Swan Society Conference.

Hayward, C. L., C. Cottam, A. M. Woodbury, and H. H. Frost. 1976. Birds of Utah. Great Basin Naturalist Memoirs. Number 1. Brigham Young University Press. Provo, Utah. 229 pp.

Reed, T. 2000. 2000 Fall Trumpeter Swan survey. U.S. Fish and Wildlife Service, Red Rocks Lakes National Wildlife Refuge, Lima, Montana. 9pp. (Plus Figures and Tables).

Gritman, J. C. 1991. Keynote Address: Twelfth Trumpeter Swan Society Conference. Pages 3-4 in J. V. Englund, ed. Proceedings and papers of the twelfth Trumpeter Swan Society Conference.

Hartwig, W. L. 1989. Memorandum from Assistant Director - Refuges and Wildlife to Regional Directors, Regions 1-8, Subject: "Trumpeter Swan Policy." U.S. Fish and Wildlife Service, Washington, DC.

Olson, D. 2001. Mid-winter survey of the Rocky Mountain Population of Trumpeter Swans. U.S. Fish and Wildlife Service, Red Rocks Lakes National Wildlife Refuge, Lima, Montana. 7pp. (Plus Figures and Tables).

Patten, M. A. and M. T. Heindel. 1994. Identifying trumpeter and tundra swans. Birding 29:306-318.

Rupp, S.P., W.B. Ballard, and M.C. Wallace. 2000. Nationwide evaluation of deer hunter harvest survey techniques. Wildl. Soc. Bull. 28(3):570-578.

Rusch, D. H., S. R. Craven, R. E. Trost, J. R. Cary, R. E. Drieslein, J. W. Ellis, and J. Wetzel. 1985. Evaluation of efforts to redistribute Canada geese. Trans. N. Amer. Wildl. Conf. 50:506-524.

Schmidt, P. 2000. Challenges in conserving swans and other migratory birds into the next millennium. North American Swans 29:41-43.

Shea, R. E. and R. C. Drewien. 1999. Evaluation of efforts to redistribute the Rocky Mountain Population of Trumpeter swans, 1986-97. Unpublished report. 51pp. (Plus Figures and Tables).

Subcommittee on Rocky Mountain Trumpeter Swans. 1998. Pacific Flyway management plan for the Rocky Mountain Population of Trumpeter Swans. Pacific Flyway Study Committee [c/o Pacific Flyway Representative, USFWS, Portland, OR], Portland, OR. 74pp.

Subcommittee on Whistling Swans. 1983. Pacific Flyway management plan for the Western Population of whistling swans. Pacific Flyway Study Comm. [c/o USFWS, MBMO] Portland, Oreg. Unpubl. rept.

Taylor, C.E., D.L. Otis, H.S. Hill, Jr., and C.R. Ruth. 2000. Design and evaluation of mail surveys to estimate deer harvest parameters. Wildl. Soc. Bull. 28(3): 717-723.

Trost, R. E., M. S. Drut, S. H. Bouffard, J. E. Cornely, J. B. Bortner, and D. Gomez. 2000. Evaluation of: Environmental Assessment: Proposal to establish general swan hunting seasons in parts of the Pacific Flyway for the 1995-99 seasons. U.S. Fish and Wildlife Service, Division of Migratory Bird Management. 14pp. (Plus Tables and Figures).

Trost, R. E., R. J. Blohm, and J. Andrew. 2000. Supplemental Environmental Assessment: Proposal to establish operational general swan hunting seasons in the Pacific Flyway. USFWS. 35pp. (Plus appendices)

USDI. 1988. Final Supplemental Environmental Impact Statement: Issuance of annual regulations permitting the sport hunting of migratory birds. U.S. Fish Wildl. Serv., Wash., D.C. 339 pp.

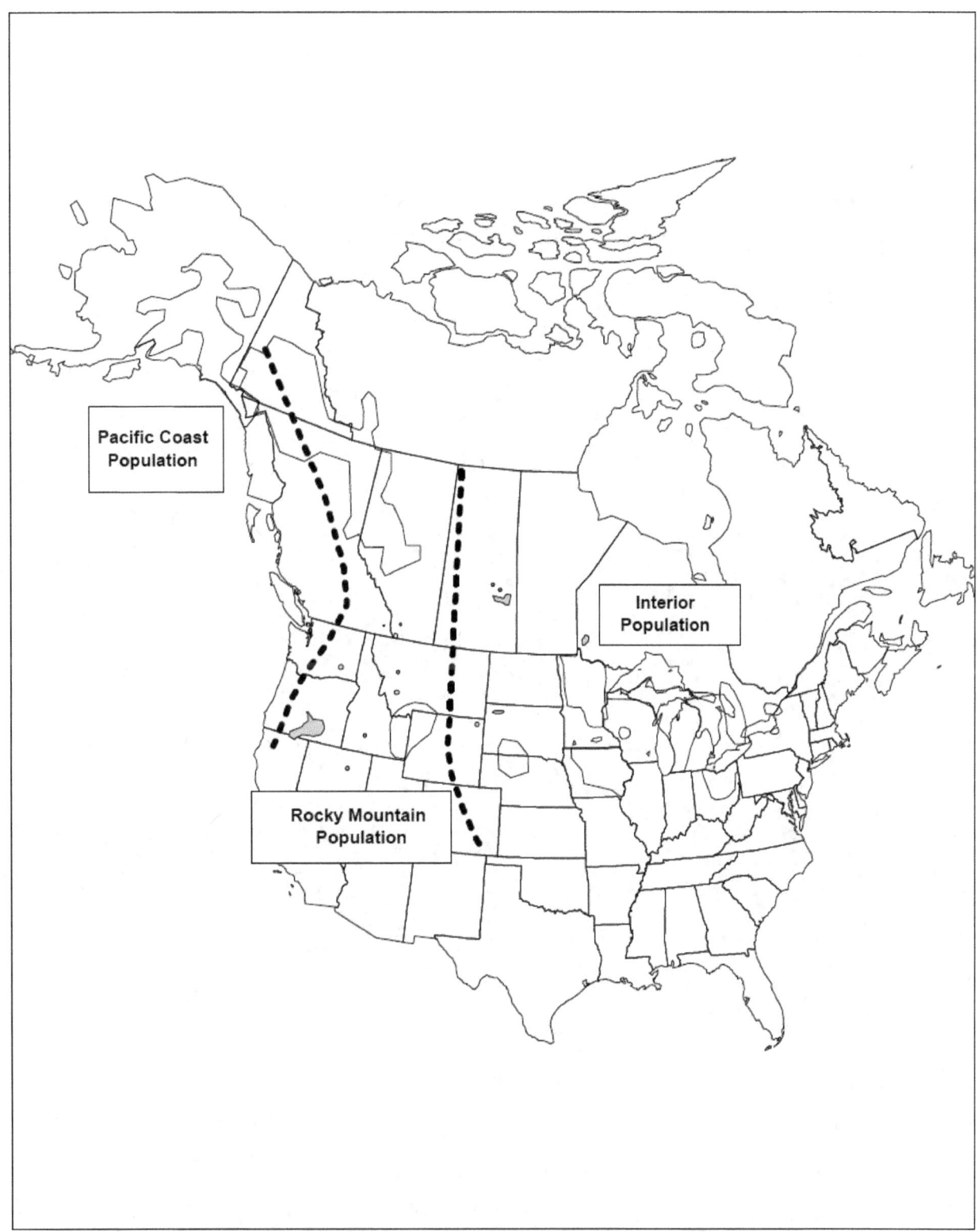

Figure 1. Approximate ranges of the 3 management populations of Trumpeter swans, Pacific, Rocky Mountain, and Interior, in North America during late-summer 2000.

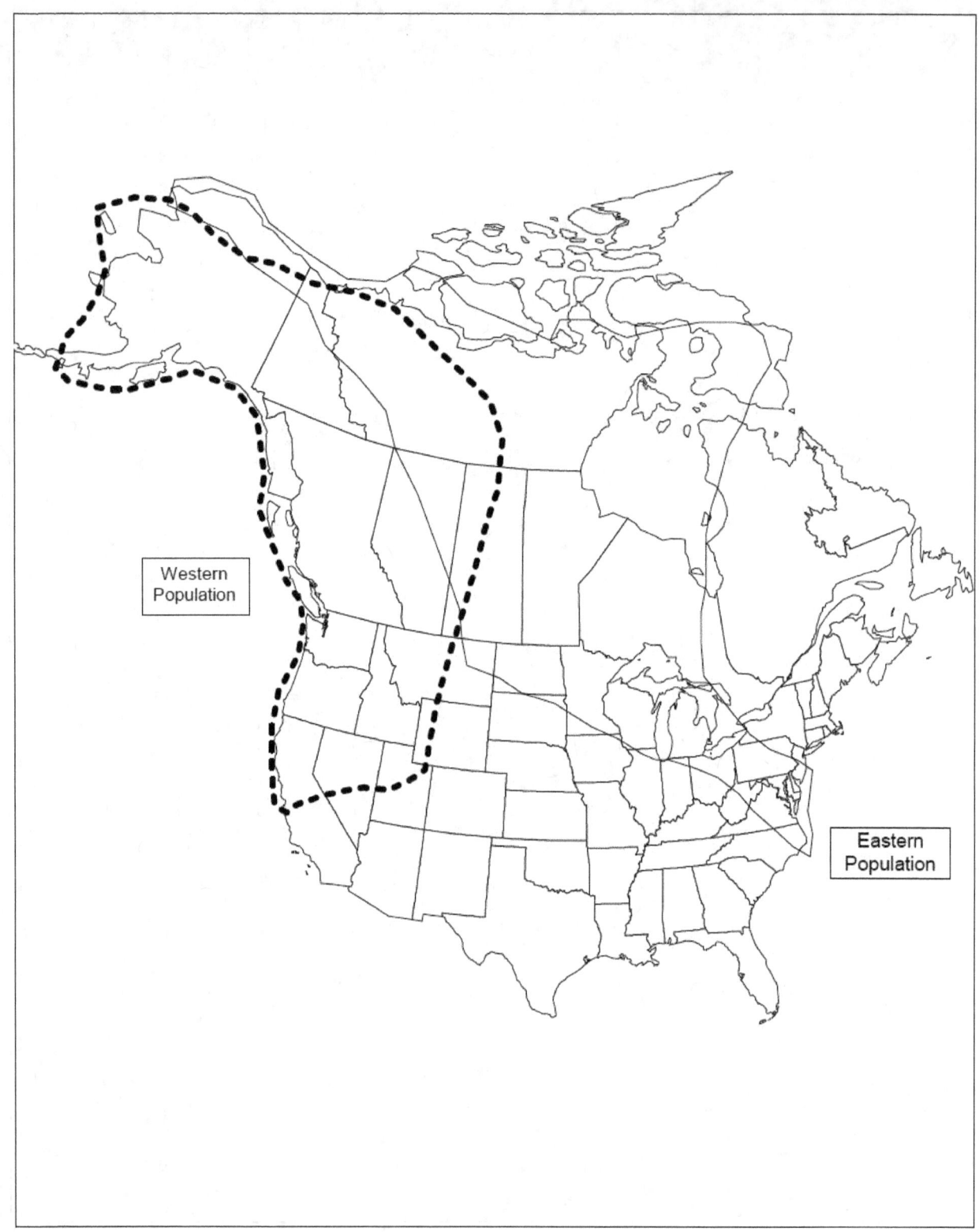

Figure 2. Approximate range of the 2 management populations of Tundra swans, Western and Eastern, in North America.

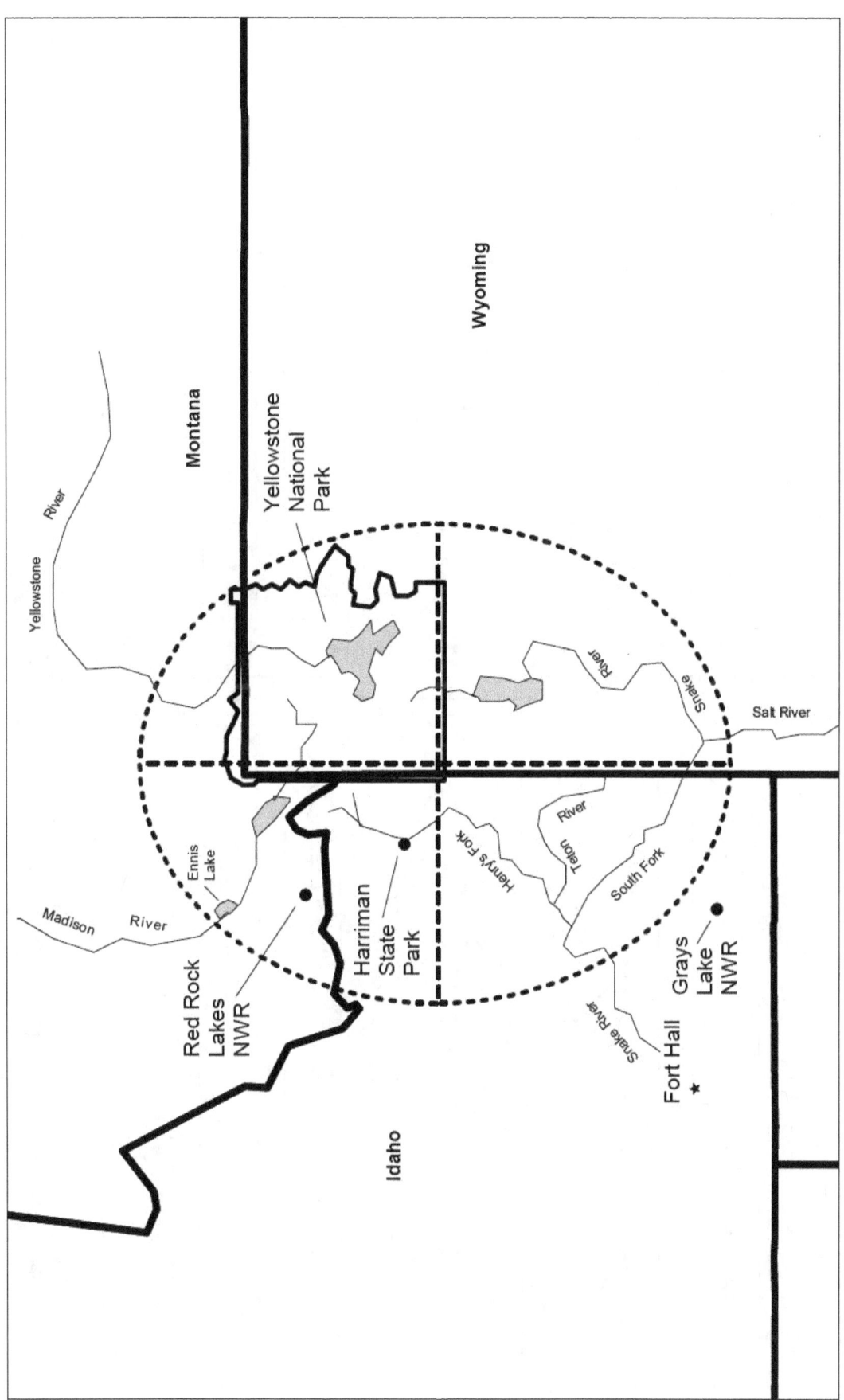

Figure 3. Tristate area of southwestern Montana, eastern Idaho, and northwestern Wyoming, with 4 quadrants delineated to assess winter trumpeter swan distribution (from Shea and Drewien 1999).

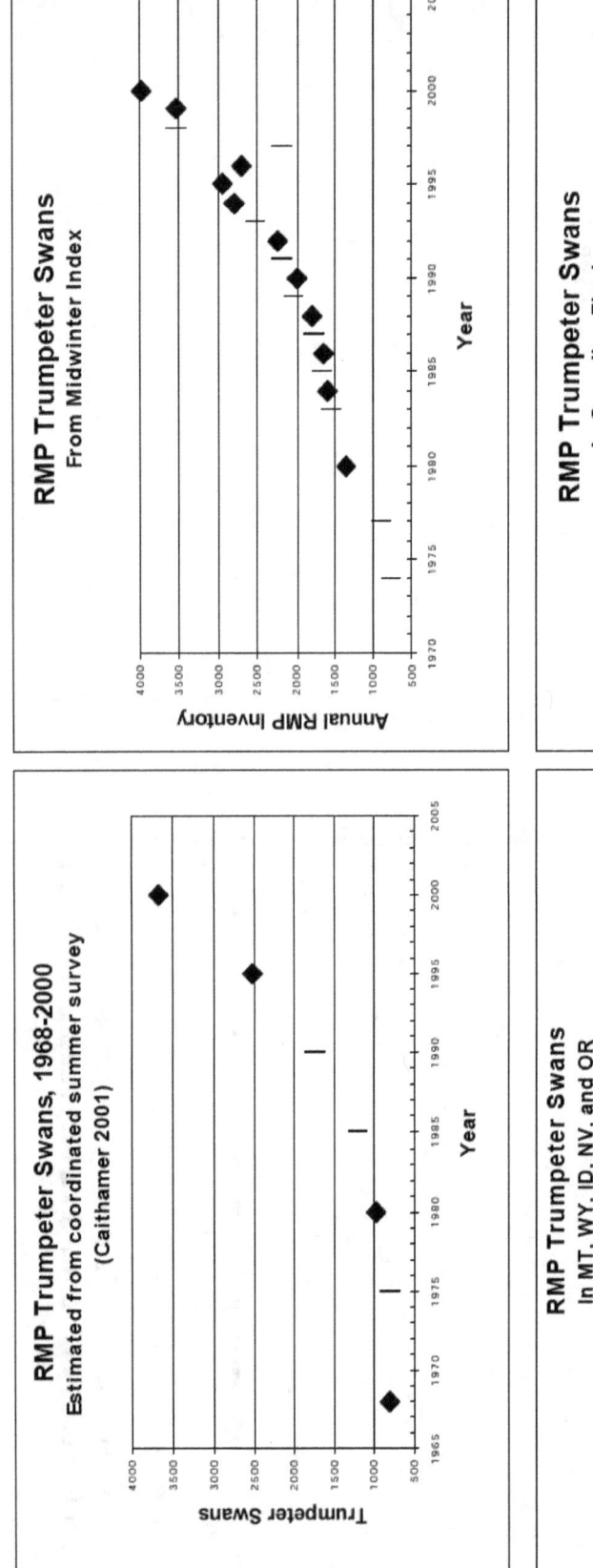

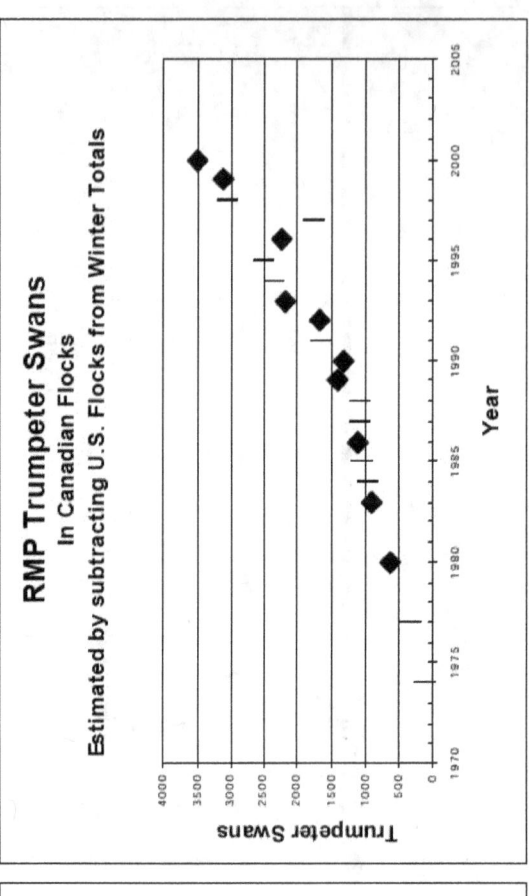

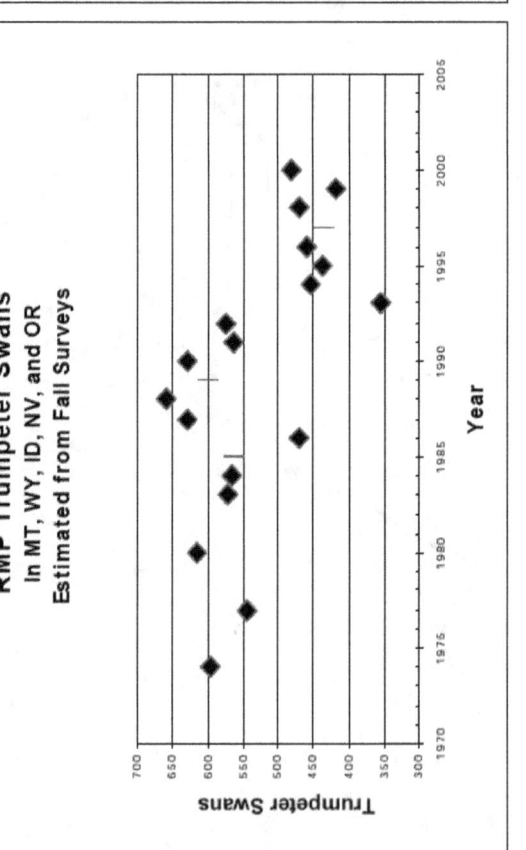

Figure 4. Estimates of RMP Trumpeter swans from the coordinated summer survey (Caithamer 2001) and the U.S. Fall and Midwinter surveys (Reed 2000, Olson 2001), 1968-2000.

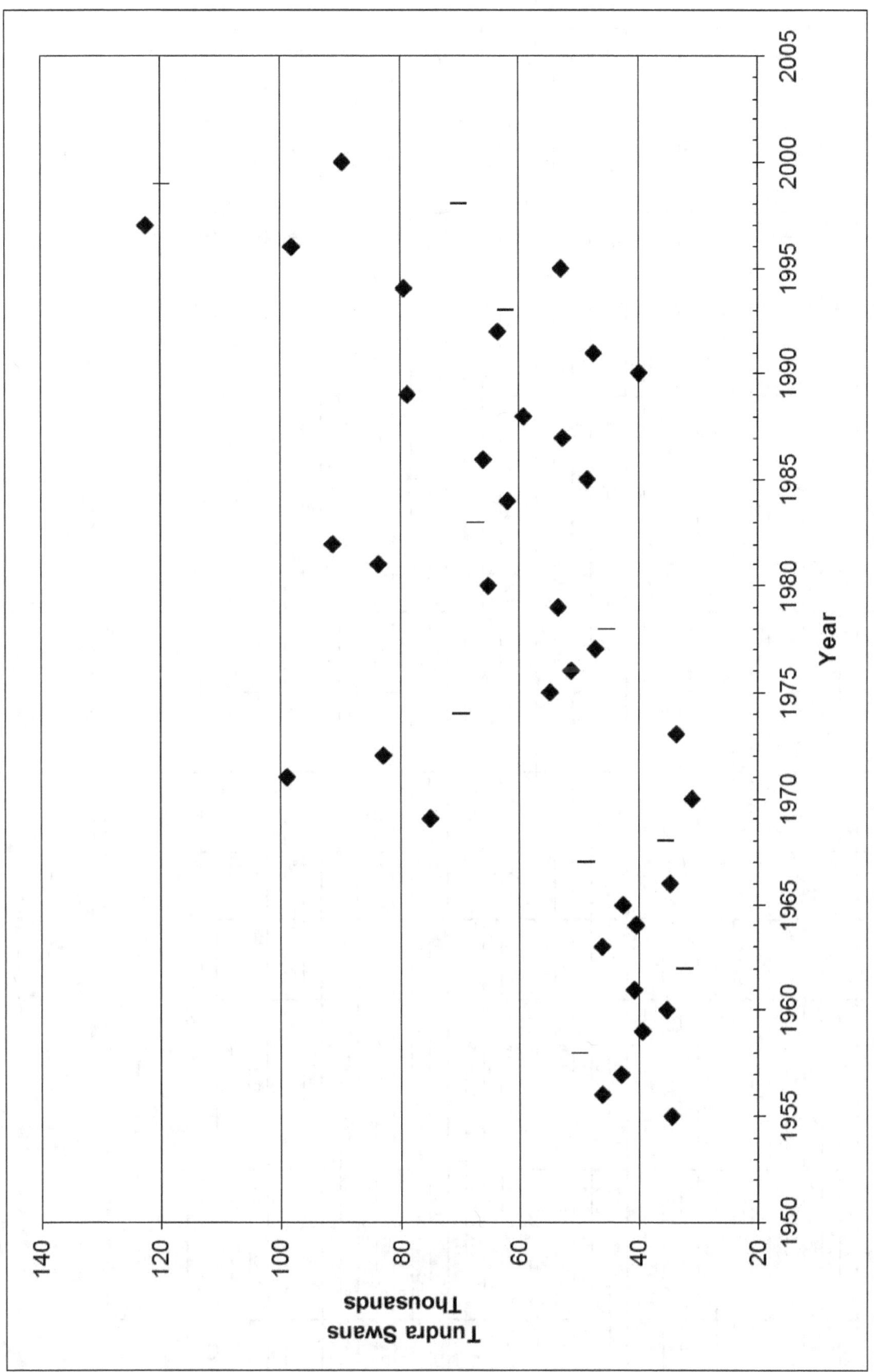

Figure 5. Estimates of western tundra swan numbers from the midwinter survey, 1955-2000.

Table 1a. Seasons, hunter participation, and harvests of the Western Population of Tundra swans in the Pacific Flyway.

| Year | Season Frameworks[a] | | | | Number of Permits | | | Active Permittees | | Hunter-days | Harvest | | | % Gray Swans in Harvest |
	Earliest Opening	Latest Closing	Concurrent w/	No./Days	Author-Ized	Applic-ation	Issued	No.	%		Retrvd	Unretrvd	Total	
1962[b]	06-Oct-62	06-Jan-63	Ducks	75	1,000	--	1,000	--	--		320	81	401	38
1963[b]	05-Oct-63	05-Jan-64	Ducks	90	1,000	1,519	1,000	--	--		392	62	454	48
1964[b]	10-Oct-64	10-Jan-65	Ducks	90	1,000	1,599	1,000	940	94	4,600	335	86	421	37
1965[b]	09-Oct-65	09-Jan-66	Ducks	90	1,000	2,495	995	915	92	4,700	336	60	396	45
1966[b]	08-Oct-66	08-Jan-67	Ducks	90	1,000	2,294	1,000	950	95	4,000	491	75	566	42
1967[b]	07-Oct-67	07-Jan-68	Ducks	90	1,000	2,766	1,000	910	91	4,800	246	69	315	54
1968[b]	05-Oct-68	12-Jan-69	Ducks	86	1,000	4,342	1,000	930	93	4,000	520	102	622	58
1969[c]	04-Oct-69	11-Jan-70	Ducks	86	3,000	6,346	3,000	2,610	87	11,410	1,377	286	1,663	62
1970[d]	03-Oct-70	17-Jan-71	Ducks	93	3,500	8,670	3,500	2,870	82	14,100	1,199	198	1,397	55
1971[d]	02-Oct-71	16-Jan-72	Ducks	93	3,500	6,833	3,495	2,806	80	13,670	1,109	193	1,302	33
1972[d]	Sat. Clst Oct l	Sun. Clst Jan 20	Ducks	93	3,500	7,634	3,500	2,520	72	13,854	1,028	132	1,160	36
1973[d]	Sat. Clst Oct l	Sun. Clst Jan 20	Ducks	93	3,500	6,805	3,500	2,780	79	11,605	1,191	257	1,448	49
1974[d]	Sat. Clst Oct l	Sun. Clst Jan 20	Ducks	93	3,500	8,431	3,500	2,935	84	13,977	1,377	298	1,675	43
1975[d]	Sat. Clst Oct l	Sun. Clst Jan 20	Ducks	93	3,500	10,180	3,500	2,915	83	13,069	1,383	241	1,624	40
1976[d]	Sat. Clst Oct l	Sun. Clst Jan 20	Ducks	93	3,500	10,163	3,500	2,940	84	12,032	1,109	164	1,273	40
1977[d]	Sat. Clst Oct l	Sun. Clst Jan 20	Ducks	93	3,500	9,413	3,488	3,035	87	10,613	1,575	347	1,922	51
1978[d]	Sat. Clst Oct l	Sun. Clst Jan 20	Ducks	93	3,500	10,985	3,500	2,870	82	10,622	1,152	375	1,527	44
1979[d]	Sat. Clst Oct l	Sun. Clst Jan 20	Ducks	93	3,500	9,661	3,500	2,930	84	11,551	1,293	345	1,638	39
1980[d]	Sat. Clst Oct l	Sun. Clst Jan 20	Ducks	93	3,500	10,943	3,500	2,895	83	10,950	1,156	223	1,379	48
1981[e]	Sat. Clst Oct l	Sun. Clst Jan 20	Ducks	93	3,500	7,798	3,500	3,000	86	10,756	1,619	377	1,996	36
1982[e]	Sat. Clst Oct l	Sun. Clst Jan 20	Ducks	93	3,500	8,385	3,500	2,940	84	12,743	1,244	311	1,555	36
1983[f]	Sat. Clst Oct l	Sun. Clst Jan 20	Ducks	93	3,650	6,848	3,650	3,007	82	12,452	1,168	286	1,454	43
1984[f]	Sat. Clst Oct l	Sun. Clst Jan 20	Ducks	93	3,650	6,259	3,650	2,949	81	13,037	1,194	126	1,320	38
1985[f]	08-Oct-85	13-Jan-86	Ducks	79	3,650	5,991	3,645	2,731	75	13,527	673	97	770	32
1986[f]	04-Oct-86	11-Jan-87	Ducks	79	3,650	4,246	3,608	2,825	78	12,884	947	185	1,132	37
1987[f]	03-Oct-87	10-Jan-88	Ducks	79	3,650	3,944	3,593	2,723	76	13,519	600	66	666	33
1988[g]	Sat. Clst Oct l	Sun. Clst Jan 20	n/a	93	3,950	2,841	3,372	2,496	74	9,656	854	123	977	36
1989[h]	Sat. Clst Oct l	Sun. Clst Jan 20	n/a	93	3,950	2,920	3,454	2,668	77	10,330	1,093	193	1,286	37
1990[h]	Sat. Clst Oct l	Sun. Clst Jan 20	n/a	93	3,950	3,497	3,378	2,698	80	10,199	1,231	177	1,408	32
1991[h]	Sat. Clst Oct l	Sun. Clst Jan 20	n/a	93	3,950	4,302	3,342	2,369	71	9,769	923	168	1,091	42
1992[h]	Sat. Clst Oct l	Sun. Clst Jan 20	n/a	93	3,950	4,032	3,189	2,369	74	10,696	716	50	766	30
1993[i]	Sat. Clst Oct l	Sun. Clst Jan 20	n/a	100	4,450	4,176	3,375	2,625	78	14,409	700	76	776	29
1994[i]	Sat. Clst Oct l	Varies[j]	n/a	100	4,450	4,715	3,422	2,784	81	11,279	1,212	153	1,365	39
1995[j]	Sat. Clst Oct l	Varies[k]	n/a	79	4,700	5,177	3,843	2,921	76	14,997	649	104	753	31
1996[j]	Sat. Clst Oct l	Varies[k]	n/a	79	4,700	4,584	3,819	3,246	85	12,698	1,353	284	1,637	35
1997[j]	Sat. Clst Oct l	Varies[k]	n/a	79	4,700	5,329	3,835	3,260	85	12,826	1,188	216	1,404	24
1998[j]	Sat. Clst Oct l	Varies[k]	n/a	79	5,000	5,560	3,934	3,344	85	11,973	1,642	308	1,950	26
1999[j]	Sat. Clst Oct l	Varies[k]	n/a	79	5,000	6,717	3,995	3,316	83	11,485	1,387	236	1,623	21
2000[j]	Sat. Clst Oct l	Varies[l]	n/a	79	5,000	5,869	2,993	2,579	80	11,054	849	141	990	39
Avg.				89	3,150	5,902	3,132	2,577	82	11,054	996	186	1,182	39

[a] Framework dates and season lengths apply to Utah, Nevada, and Montana. Alaska frameworks are from September 1 through January 29, with 107 days.

[b] Hunting in Utah (statewide).

[c] Hunting in Utah (statewide); Nevada (Churchill Co.).

[d] Hunting in Utah (statewide); Nevada (Churchill Co.); Montana (Teton Co.).

[e] Hunting in Utah (statewide); Nevada (Churchill Co.); Montana (Teton and Cascade Cos.).

[f] Hunting in Utah (statewide); Nevada (Churchill, Lyon, and Pershing Cos.); Montana (Teton and Cascade Cos.).

[g] Hunting in Utah (statewide); Nevada (Churchill, Lyon, and Pershing Cos.); Montana (Teton, Cascade, Toole, Liberty, Hill, and Pondera Cos.); Alaska (GMU 22).

[h] Hunting in Utah (statewide, except for Cache, Rich, Daggett, and Unitah Cos.); Nevada (Churchill, Lyon, and Pershing Cos.); Montana (Teton, Cascade, Toole, Liberty, Hill, and Pondera Cos.); Alaska (GMU 22 and 18).

[i] Utah season ends by Dec. 15. Elsewhere, Sunday Closest to Jan. 20.

[j] Hunting in Utah (Great Salt Lake Basin); Nevada (Churchill, Lyon, and Pershing Cos.); Montana (Cascade, Chouteau, Hill, Liberty, Toole, and portions of Pondera and Teton Cos.).

[k] Utah season ends first Sunday in Dec.; Nevada season ends first Sunday after Jan. 1; Montana season ends no later than Dec. 1.

[l] Utah season ends second Sunday in Dec.; Nevada season ends first Sunday after Jan. 1; Montana season ends no later than Dec. 1.

Table 1b. Seasons, hunter participation, and harvests of the Western Population of Tundra swans in Montana (Pacific Flyway).

Year	Seasons			Number of Permits			Active Permittees		Hunter-days	Harvest			% Gray Swans in Harvest
	Opening	Closing	No. Days	Authorized	Application	Issued	No.	%		Retrvd	Unretrvd	Total	
1970 [a]	10-Oct	10-Jan	93	500	500	500	275	55	1,130	179	--	179	41
1971 [a]	09-Oct	09-Jan	93	500	500	500	245	49	1,128	91	--	91	33
1972 [a]	01-Oct	01-Jan	93	500	500	500	265	53	1,122	150	--	150	31
1973 [a]	06-Oct	06-Jan	93	500	500	500	230	46	757	101	11	112	45
1974 [a]	28-Sep	29-Dec	93	500	500	500	350	70	1,217	259	56	315	48
1975 [a]	04-Oct	04-Jan	93	500	500	500	350	70	874	266	37	303	34
1976 [a]	02-Oct	02-Jan	93	500	500	500	380	76	969	139	12	151	43
1977 [a]	01-Oct	01-Jan	93	500	500	500	--	--	--	214	26	240	35
1978 [a]	30-Sep	31-Dec	93	500	500	500	350	70	571	146	19	165	37
1979 [a]	29-Sep	30-Dec	93	500	500	500	390	78	1,119	275	62	337	32
1980 [a]	04-Oct	04-Jan	93	500	500	500	400	80	965	250	22	272	41
1981 [b]	03-Oct	03-Jan	93	500	500	500	330	66	703	177	17	194	30
1982 [b]	02-Oct	02-Jan	93	500	500	500	340	68	799	139	9	148	27
1983 [b]	01-Oct	01-Jan	93	500	500	500	375	75	931	218	17	235	40
1984 [b]	29-Sep	30-Dec	93	500	500	500	305	61	414	221	6	227	25
1985 [b]	12-Oct	29-Dec	79	500	500	500	275	55	596	185	12	197	21
1986 [b]	04-Oct	21-Dec	79	500	500	500	270	54	756	200	16	216	26
1987 [b]	03-Oct	20-Dec	79	500	500	500	395	79	829	280	23	303	32
1988 [c]	01-Oct	01-Jan	93	500	500	500	355	71	722	260	19	279	29
1989 [c]	30-Sep	31-Dec	93	500	500	500	400	80	779	302	38	340	29
1990 [c]	29-Sep	30-Dec	93	500	500	500	370	74	749	275	20	295	27
1991 [c]	12-Oct	29-Dec	79	500	500	500	185	37	444	79	7	86	35
1992 [c]	17-Oct	03-Jan	79	500	500	500	365	73	817	221	6	227	20
1993 [c]	16-Oct	02-Jan	79	500	500	500	380	76	1,191	290	28	318	30
1994 [c]	15-Oct	01-Jan	79	500	500	500	405	81	730	326	24	350	27
1995 [d]	14-Oct	01-Dec	49	500	500	500	340	68	765	182	13	195	30
1996 [d]	12-Oct	01-Dec	51	500	500	500	415	83	843	302	23	325	22
1997 [d]	18-Oct	01-Dec	45	500	500	500	395	79	709	300	57	357	24
1998 [d]	17-Oct	01-Dec	46	500	500	500	415	83	917	276	47	323	20
1999 [d]	16-Oct	01-Dec	47	500	500	500	390	78	1,033	226	13	239	17
2000 [d]	14-Oct	01-Dec	49	500	500	500	360	72	670	217	29	246	17
Avg:	06-Oct	25-Dec	81	500	834	500	343	69	842	218	24	239	31

[a] Hunting in only Teton County.

[b] Hunting in only Teton and Cascade counties.

[c] Hunting in only Teton, Cascade, Toole, Liberty, Hill, and Pondera counties.

[d] Hunting in only Choteau, Cascade, Toole, Liberty, Hill, and portions of Teton and Pondera counties.

Table 1c. Seasons, hunter participation, and harvests of the Western Population of Tundra swans in Nevada.

Year	Seasons			Number of Permits			Active Permittees		Hunter-days	Harvest			% Gray Swans in Harvest
	Opening	Closing	No. Days	Author-ized	Applic-ation	Issued	No.	%		Retr'vd	Unretr'vd	Total	
1969 [a]	01-Nov	28-Dec	58	500	--[c]	500	--	--	1,410	87	20	107	63
1970 [a]	31-Oct	03-Jan	65	500	--[c]	500	--	--	1,370	208	28	236	49
1971 [a]	06-Nov	02-Jan	58	500	510	500	415	83	1,475	102	18	120	37
1972 [a]	04-Nov	07-Jan	65	500	571	500	400	80	1,635	124	14	138	34
1973 [a]	03-Nov	06-Jan	65	500	686	500	375	75	1,315	109	10	119	47
1974 [a]	02-Nov	12-Jan	72	500	534	500	385	77	1,455	190	25	215	39
1975 [a]	01-Nov	04-Jan	65	500	690	500	390	78	1,123	188	35	223	38
1976 [a]	30-Oct	02-Jan	65	500	682	500	410	82	1,378	206	21	227	34
1977 [a]	05-Nov	15-Jan	72	500	638	500	380	76	1,326	84	10	94	46
1978 [a]	04-Nov	07-Jan	65	500	621	500	370	74	1,407	90	4	94	47
1979 [a]	03-Nov	13-Jan	72	500	604	500	390	78	1,314	214	42	256	32
1980 [a]	01-Nov	04-Jan	65	500	767	500	395	79	1,428	103	16	119	31
1981 [a]	07-Nov	10-Jan	65	500	500	500	445	89	1,115	301	49	350	32
1982 [b]	23-Oct	09-Jan	79	500	534	500	400	80	1,200	161	22	183	20
1983 [b]	22-Oct	08-Jan	79	650	650	650	507	78	1,833	169	24	193	29
1984 [b]	20-Oct	06-Jan	79	650	650	650	494	76	1,618	229	22	251	31
1985 [b]	19-Oct	29-Dec	72	650	650	650	436	67	1,381	145	12	157	34
1986 [b]	18-Oct	04-Jan	79	650	608	608	480	79	1,530	196	58	254	34
1987 [b]	17-Oct	03-Jan	79	650	594	594	404	68	1,694	94	11	105	38
1988 [b]	08-Oct	08-Jan	93	650	260	260	195	75	770	78	4	82	49
1989 [b]	14-Oct	14-Jan	93	650	324	324	262	81	1,076	81	4	85	37
1990 [b]	20-Oct	20-Jan	93	650	297	297	232	78	994	67	6	73	36
1991 [b]	19-Oct	19-Jan	93	650	258	258	181	70	721	62	2	64	47
1992 [b]	17-Oct	17-Jan	93	650	100	100	71	71	242	29	2	31	36
1993 [b]	16-Oct	23-Jan	100	650	205	205	135	66	668	55	3	58	31
1994 [b]	15-Oct	22-Jan	100	650	206	206	161	78	601	88	7	95	43
1995 [b]	21-Oct	07-Jan	79	650	383	383	287	75	1,224	72	20	92	41
1996 [b]	19-Oct	05-Jan	79	650	376	376	331	88	1,054	119	17	136	37
1997 [b]	18-Oct	04-Jan	79	650	381	381	328	86	1,282	131	16	147	38
1998 [b]	17-Oct	03-Jan	79	650	492	492	418	85	1,552	185	24	209	16
1999 [b]	16-Oct	02-Jan	79	650	518	518	435	84	1,817	212	19	231	31
2000 [b]	21-Oct	07-Jan	79	650	509	493	360	73	1,214	82	7	89	41
Avg:	21-Dec	23-Feb	77	584	493	451	349	78	1,257	133	18	151	37

[a] Hunting in only Churchill County.

[b] Hunting in only Churchill, Lyon, and Pershing Counties.

[c] Permits provided on a first-come, first-served basis.

Table 1d. Seasons, hunter participation, and harvests of the Western Population of Tundra swans in Utah.

Year	Seasons Opening	Seasons Closing	Seasons No. Days	Number of Permits Authorized	Number of Permits Issued	Number of Permits Application	Active Permittees No.	Active Permittees %	Hunter-days	Harvest Retrvd	Harvest Unretrvd	Harvest Total	% Gray Swans in Harvest
1962	20-Oct	26-Dec	68	1,000	1,000	--ᵃ	--	--	--	320	81	401	38
1963	05-Oct	02-Jan	90	1,000	1,000	1,519	--	--	--	392	62	454	48
1964	10-Oct	07-Jan	90	1,000	1,000	1,599	940	94	4,600	335	86	421	37
1965	09-Oct	06-Jan	90	1,000	995	2,495	915	92	4,700	336	60	396	45
1966	08-Oct	05-Jan	90	1,000	1,000	2,294	950	95	4,800	491	75	566	42
1967	07-Oct	04-Jan	90	1,000	1,000	2,766	910	91	4,800	246	69	315	54
1968	12-Oct	05-Jan	86	1,000	1,000	4,342	930	93	4,300	520	102	622	58
1969	11-Oct	04-Jan	86	2,500	2,500	6,346	2,225	89	10,000	1,290	266	1,556	62
1970	03-Oct	03-Jan	93	2,500	2,500	7,670	2,200	88	11,600	812	170	982	52
1971	02-Oct	02-Jan	93	2,500	2,495	5,823	2,146	86	11,067	916	175	1,091	33
1972	07-Oct	07-Jan	93	2,500	2,500	6,563	2,100	84	11,097	754	118	872	38
1973	06-Oct	06-Jan	93	2,500	2,500	5,619	2,175	87	9,533	981	236	1,217	50
1974	05-Oct	05-Jan	93	2,500	2,500	7,397	2,200	88	11,305	928	217	1,145	42
1975	04-Oct	04-Jan	93	2,500	2,500	8,874	2,175	87	11,072	929	169	1,098	46
1976	02-Oct	02-Jan	93	2,500	2,500	8,877	2,150	86	9,685	764	131	895	41
1977	01-Oct	01-Jan	93	2,500	2,488	8,097	2,264	91	8,411	1,277	311	1,588	54
1978	07-Oct	07-Jan	93	2,500	2,500	9,574	2,150	86	8,635	916	352	1,268	45
1979	06-Oct	06-Jan	93	2,500	2,500	8,349	2,150	86	9,118	804	241	1,045	43
1980	04-Oct	04-Jan	93	2,500	2,500	9,264	2,100	84	8,557	803	185	988	52
1981	03-Oct	03-Jan	93	2,500	2,500	6,326	2,225	89	8,938	1,141	311	1,452	38
1982	02-Oct	02-Jan	93	2,500	2,500	7,112	2,200	88	10,744	944	280	1,224	40
1983	08-Oct	08-Jan	93	2,500	2,500	5,509	2,125	85	9,688	781	245	1,026	47
1984	13-Oct	06-Jan	86	2,500	2,500	5,008	2,150	86	11,005	744	98	842	44
1985	12-Oct	29-Dec	79	2,500	2,495	4,693	2,021	81	11,550	343	73	416	37
1986	04-Oct	21-Dec	79	2,500	2,500	2,933	2,075	83	10,598	551	111	662	42
2-way splitᵇ													
1987	08-Oct	01-Jan	79	2,500	2,499	2,509	1,924	77	10,996	226	32	258	33
1988	07-Oct	02-Jan	86	2,500	2,500	1,772	1,875	75	8,164	501	100	601	37
1989	06-Oct	06-Jan	88	2,500	2,500	1,599	1,925	77	8,475	694	146	840	40
1990	05-Oct	05-Jan	93	2,500	2,500	2,201	2,050	82	8,456	874	151	1,025	33
1991	05-Oct	05-Jan	93	2,500	2,500	3,096	1,950	78	8,304	774	159	933	42
1992	03-Oct	03-Jan	93	2,500	2,500	3,039	1,875	75	9,405	450	42	492	31
1993	02-Oct	03-Jan	94	2,500	2,500	3,041	2,025	81	12,550	337	41	378	28
1994ᶜ	08-Oct	15-Dec	69	2,500	2,500	3,469	2,100	84	9,948	768	120	888	29
1995ᵈ	07-Oct	03-Dec	58	2,750	2,750	3,496	2,173	79	13,008	348	70	418	41
1996ᵈ	05-Oct	01-Dec	58	2,750	2,750	2,941	2,393	87	10,801	897	241	1,138	31
1997ᵈ	04-Oct	07-Dec	65	2,750	2,750	3,449	2,393	87	10,835	704	193	897	35
1998ᵈ	03-Oct	06-Dec	65	2,750	2,750	3,312	2,420	88	9,504	1,142	283	1,425	25
1999ᵈ	02-Oct	05-Dec	65	2,750	2,750	4,325	2,338	85	8,637	858	212	1,070	26
2000ᵉ	07-Oct	10-Dec	65	2,000	2,000	3,913	1,680	84	8,025	550	105	655	19
Avg:	06-Oct	29-Dec	85	2,250	2,249	4,769	1,962	85	9,246	704	157	861	40

ᵃ Permits provided on a first-come, first-served basis.
ᵇ Oct.3-Dec.6 & Dec.21-Jan.3.
ᶜ Statewide, except for Cache, Rich, Daggett, and Uintah Cos. & season ends by Dec.15.
ᵈ Great Salt Lake Basin only & season ends on first Sunday in Dec.
ᵉ Great Salt Lake Basin only & season ends on second Sunday in Dec.

Table 2. Swan Harvest, Reporting Statistics, and Estimated Trumpeter Harvest in the Pacific Flyway, 1994-2000.

YEAR	Tundra Swan Harvest Estimates			Swans Examined			Compliance Rate [a]			Trumpeters Detected [b]		
	Utah	Nevada	Montana	Utah	Nevada	Montana	Utah	Nevada	Montana	Utah[c]	Nevada	Montana
1994	768	88	326	474	78	219	61.7%	88.6%	67.2%	0	0	1
1995	348	72	182	244	66	110	70.1%	91.7%	60.4%	3	0	3
1996	897	119	302	701	110	181	78.1%	92.4%	59.9%	7	1	3
1997	704	131	300	497	116	217	70.6%	88.5%	72.3%	3	0	1
1998	1,142	185	276	879	156	168	77.0%	84.3%	60.9%	1	0	3
1999	858	212	226	647	186	153	75.4%	87.7%	67.7%	0	0	7
2000	550	82[d]	217	454	65	203	82.5%	79.3%	93.5%	1	0	3
TOTAL	5,267	889	1,829	3,896	777	1,251	74.0%	87.4%	68.4%	15	1	21

[a] Compliance Rate = Swans Examined/Expanded Tundra Swan Harvest Estimate.

[b] Criteria for Trumpeter Detection = Ad w/o yellow lore and posterior nare to bill tip > or = 62mm, Juv w/o yellow lore and posterior nare to bill tip > or = 61mm.

[c] In 1996, 6 of the 7 trumpeters detected in Utah's harvest were swans marked and translocated from Idaho and released in Utah as part of a research proposal. The other was a marked swan that was translocated from Idaho to Oregon 2 years earlier.

[d] 2000 harvest estimates in Nevada may be subject to some minor adjustment due to late survey responses. Any such changes will be minor and will not alter conclusions regarding the number of trumpeter swans harvested.

www.ingramcontent.com/pod-product-compliance
Lightning Source LLC
Chambersburg PA
CBHW080547290526
45790CB00006B/2582